OCEAN FEVER

THE DAMIAN FOXALL STORY

Damian Foxall
with David Branigan

The Collins Press

FIRST PUBLISHED IN 2011 BY
The Collins Press
West Link Park
Doughcloyne
Wilton
Cork

© Damian Foxall and David Branigan 2011

Damian Foxall and David Branigan have asserted their moral right to
be identified as the authors of this work.

British Library Cataloguing in Publication Data

Foxall, Damian
   Ocean fever.
   1. Foxall, Damian. 2. Sailors—Ireland—Biography.
   3. Sailboat racing.
   I. Title II. Branigan, David.
   797.1'4'092-dc22

ISBN-13: 978-1-84889-037-4

Typesetting by Patricia Hope, Dublin
Typeset in Sabon
Printed in Italy by 🦁 Grafica Veneta S.p.A.

Cover photographs
Front: Damian Foxall during sea trials with the French team for the
2011–2012 Volvo Ocean Race. (Yvan Zedda)
Back: deep in the Southern Ocean on board *Team Tyco* during the
2001–2002 Volvo Ocean Race. (Foxall family)
Spine and inside back: Damian Foxall, 2011. (Pilpre Arnaud)
Inside front: Damian Foxall on *Ericsson*, Volvo Ocean Race 2005–2006.
(David Branigan/Oceansport)

Contents

World Map   viii
Acknowledgements   xi

1 Knights of the *Green Dragon*   1

2 Coming to Ireland   53

3 The Derrynane Years   65

4 London Calling   94

5 Sun, Sand, Sea and Sailing   113

6 La Vie en France   141

7 Racing the World   165

8 The World Turned Upside Down   200

9 Non-stop, Never Give Up   220

Appendix
Round-The-World Races   273

The *Ocean Fever* stories are all true though some individuals' names have been changed for reasons of privacy. Dialogue has been included from best recollection.

Map of the World

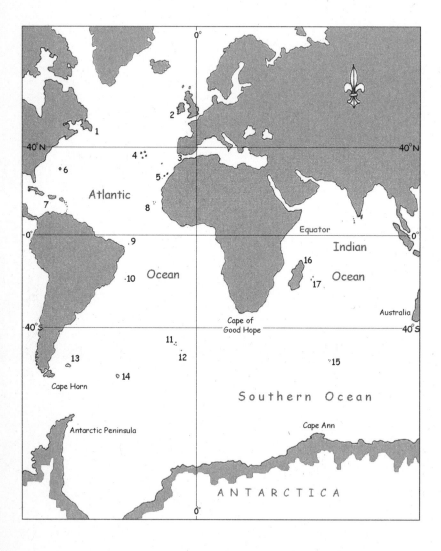

1. Newfoundland
2. Derrynane, Ireland
3. Strait of Gibraltar
4. Azores
5. Canary Islands
6. Bermuda

7. Caribbean Sea
8. Cape Verde Islands
9. Fernando de Noronha
10. Martim Vaz
11. Tristan da Cunha Grp
12. Gough Island

13. Falkland Islands
14. South Georgia
15. Kerguelen Islands
16. Madagascar
17. Mauritius
18. Hobart, Tasmania

19. South Island NZ
20. Chatham Islands
21. Fiji
22. Pitcairn Islands
23. Hawaiian Islands
24. Galapagos Islands

Acknowledgements

To try to acknowledge everyone connected with these stories and to thank those who helped would be an impossible task and very unfair if somebody was left out. So our gratitude goes to everyone connected, however distantly, with the *Ocean Fever* stories, especially to all the owners, skippers, crews and shore teams who make high-performance racing on the world's oceans possible.

For their patience and understanding in delivering the final copy the authors are truly grateful to: all at The Collins Press; Patricia Hope; Rosemary Dawson, ace publicist and friend; photographers Thierry Martinez, Benoît Stichelbaut and Yvan Zedda for use of their dramatic work; Kevin Murphy for his drawings; Donal Browne; Paul Gough for his sporting eye and critique; and also to everyone in Derrynane and Caherdaniel, for your constant encouragement, friendship and great humour.

Finally, and most especially, to Suzy-Ann and Jennifer for their patience and support, especially when it seemed like completing this book was all that mattered.

Damian Foxall, Lorient
David Branigan, Dun Laoghaire
2011

1

Knights of the *Green Dragon*

Volvo Ocean Race 2008

End of Leg 1: Cape Town

Billowing clouds swept around the crest of Table Mountain. The sprawling city and suburbs of Cape Town were bathed in glorious sunshine as visitors thronged the historic Victoria & Albert Waterfront in early December 2008. It was 6 a.m. and, stepping outside in running shoes, I closed the front door of our hotel apartment quietly so as not to wake my wife, Suzy-Ann, and our two-year-old son, Oisín. They were still recovering from their long flight to South Africa and it was only the beginning of a long year of travel and living out of suitcases, a roller coaster of emotion that would include disasters and successes, goodbyes and hellos at the dockside as normal life was once again put on hold for them.

I jogged through the crowds, part of the stream of professional sailors all heading to work for the day, following morning workout sessions at the gym. After three weeks at sea non-stop, the change to life ashore was very welcome. Gathered around the quays were the bases of the seven Volvo Ocean Race teams that had just arrived at the end of Leg 1 of the epic 39,000-mile race around the world after starting out from Alicante on Spain's Mediterranean coast barely three weeks earlier.

At first glance, each 70-foot yacht appeared similar, apart from the sponsors' colours and graphics that covered every inch of surface area. In fact, the boats varied hugely and were the result of years of collective effort by naval architects, engineers and various scientists even before each was built by a team comprising experts in disciplines from electronics to carbon fibre construction. The level of technology required is comparable to the aviation industry but without the passenger requirement – or the regulation.

At this point, the end of Leg 1 (out of ten) on the ultimate proving ground, the test was under way of the design and build teams and the crews pitted against one another and all, in turn, against the forces of nature across the oceans and seaways of the planet.

Each boat was craned out within hours of arrival, stripped of almost everything not bolted or bonded in place, for the planned refit and repair programmes. The previous three weeks had been punishing on both men and equipment but worse lay ahead. Preventative maintenance now would offset more serious problems later and the restaurants of the V&A were grandstands for the boatyards that had appeared overnight to herald the arrival of the fleet.

Nestling in one corner of the docks, between the slips where Chinese tuna boats were being refitted and the elegant corporate offices of the BOE Stockbrokers building, a small pier near the maritime museum that once served as the team base for the South African America's Cup Team *Shosholoza* had become the adoptive home for the *Green Dragon* team, our Sino-Irish entry in the race.

Compared to the other teams, project management had pulled off a neat coup. While all had pairs of fully fitted shipping containers and marquees leapfrogging around the world to be waiting at each destination, we had the relative luxury of a purpose-built office and dock space with workshops and sail loft ready to move into. *Green Dragon* had her own berth and the shore team had easy access from their equipment containers just yards away. Team members enjoyed desk space and rows of laptop computers with dedicated high-speed Internet access surrounded by catering-sized jars of vitamin supplements and high-energy drinks aimed at offsetting the race diet of freeze-dried fare. Work lists, calendars and performance charts covered the walls; at this early stage in the campaign, some of the data might have been of interest to rival crews and visitors were welcomed with a wariness in case sensitive information might make its way outside the tightly knit project structure.

The base was indeed a bonus, a saving of effort and precious resources but was still a pyrrhic victory of sorts. Having the use of the *Shosholoza* facility was a reminder of our underfunded campaign, which was obliged to take whatever savings could be eked out without affecting performance: our own mobile bases were as good as any

3

other team's but the expense of setting these up could wait till later in the race.

Nevertheless, an upbeat mood permeated the dockside. Local schoolkids arrived to visit the boat; Colin Wrafter, the Irish Ambassador to South Africa, toured the project in person. It was early days in a very long race and we had just delivered what appeared to be a credible result that defied the odds. The sun was shining and all appeared to be well.

On this morning, however, in the boardroom over-looking the base, a private meeting was about to take place and would review in detail everything that had taken place at sea over the past three weeks. Just like the planning that had gone into the campaign, it would be exhaustive and very thorough.

The Beginnings

We were the team that our skipper, Ian Walker, built. Or more correctly, that he and his business partner Jamie Boag built for a syndicate of Irish business people who were deeply committed to sailing and the opportunities that the Volvo Ocean Race offered the country.

As a double Olympic silver medallist, Walker had barely been out of sight of land on the Fastnet Race, such was the extent of his offshore/oceanic racing experience. In the broad church that is the sport of sailing, inshore and Olympic racing are worlds apart; and competitive ocean racing – thousands of miles from land – and inshore racing are equally distant. Yet the challenges of any yacht race and racing tactics, whether inshore or offshore, were attractive for Walker. This plus his team management ability overcame any reluctance to embark on a round-the-world race.

That Walker is one of the best inshore racing sailors around none of us had any doubt. He was certainly no pushover; you don't get to win two Olympic medals without being one of the best helmsmen in the world; he knew how to drive any boat quickly. But as skipper he had the toughest and loneliest role on board a fully crewed racing yacht at sea for weeks on end. Little wonder while we were at sea he and Boag burned up time on the sat phone as they discussed the wider issues of the project that we had been insulated from – and had insulated ourselves from. For the rest of us, our roles had little bearing on 'the big picture' and knowing this we simply immersed ourselves in being focused on the job at hand, exclusively while at sea and barely leaving time for personal lives ashore.

In spite of the rigours of his role and inexperience offshore, Walker learnt the priorities quickly. As legendary Whitbread race skippers went, the old-school mantra of 'follow-me-or-fuck-off' was successfully championed by Lawrie Smith and Grant Dalton decades earlier. Although both led from the front, able in almost every role on board, the traditional top-down hierarchical command structure has since given way to flatter management that gathers good sailors with specific expertise on board increasingly complex racing boats. Walker's coordination style was also to get stuck in himself, to be involved in all aspects of the project and was as demanding of himself as he was of everyone else. There would be no faulting him on the energy and commitment he put into the campaign and he was motivated most by excellence, both in himself and his team. To be skipper and learn all the functions of deck work was hard but mental toughness plus his considerable work rate, on top of his load of responsibilities, quickly overcame this. He confided in a small group of people, notably Neal 'Nelly' McDonald to whom he listened carefully, though the advice was not always heeded in the early stages of the project as Walker's hands were tied by the issues we were not aware of. Neither he nor Boag could share the full picture of the delicate background negotiations as sponsors were signed up, even halfway into the race.

A few years before, Walker was involved the Italian +39 America's Cup team so he was no stranger to big-boat campaigns and from the outset of the *Green Dragon* project, before the crew was assembled, he was immersed in budgets and doing the accounts. But that was a normal function of a start-up when they did not have money so all management activities were very centralised until gradually team members were employed. So he brought his neighbour Phil Allen onto the team who became the saviour of many logistical nightmares.

As well, around this time, the lack of a professional sailing culture in Ireland became apparent. Stepping from the hugely resourced Solent area around Southampton and the Isle of Wight not just to Ireland but to Galway and the west of Ireland was a culture shock. In the Solent area where the 'Cowes mafia' moniker holds some truth, the nebulous established network of professional sailing that puts friendship and loyalty firmly alongside skill was plainly absent across the pond. Putting together a project on this scale demands reliance on people you know and trust but without an established professional scene in Ireland, problems could quickly build up.

On top of the professional-level services gap in Ireland and the lack of high-end technical resources, another disparity existed between what the syndicate thought the team needed and what Walker and Boag knew was required, at least in the early stages of planning. The twenty years from the previous Irish entry in this race, *NCB Ireland* in the 1989–1990 Whitbread Round-the-World Race, to the present era was evident in many ways. And therein lay a problem that faced Walker and Boag.

As so many years had elapsed since a sailing project on this scale was undertaken in Ireland, the people involved had moved on, taking their knowledge and experience with them, leaving the marginal interest and more than a little cynicism that followed the outcome of that earlier race. In those days, to keep people happy, simply completing the course, safely and without serious injury, flying the Irish flag around the world in an era that pre-dated *Riverdance* just was not enough; only outright victory would do, it seemed.

Undaunted by this backdrop, almost twenty years later the syndicate behind the *Green Dragon* committed to Walker and Boag that a new boat would be designed and built, a campaign would be funded and, separately, the city of Galway would host a stopover in the closing stages of the 2008–2009 Volvo Ocean Race.

We did not appreciate it at the time but a massive leap of faith had been taken to begin building *Green Dragon* and the catalyst for this was the drive of the project's founders:

Eamon Conneely, John Killeen and Enda O'Coineen, all three passionate about sailing and Galway in equal measure.

On one of his first visits to Ireland, Walker was given a copy of Tim Pat Coogan's book *Ireland in the 20th Century*. After his introduction with the long and tortuous history between Ireland and Britain, Walker's conclusion was: 'we really fucked you guys over.' But he continued as he began, the British skipper of an Irish boat that would fly a tricolour around the world.

'This is an Irish-International team,' both Walker and Boag said at the start and that was good enough as far as we were concerned. It was an ethos that held true from beginning to end. There would be no compromising on people or materials. Where possible, Irish sailors and support crew would be employed but only if their skills fitted the requirements as it was intended to showcase Ireland in a top-class campaign.

After returning from winning the Barcelona World Race with Jean-Pierre Dick, I found the prospect of competing as a watch leader on the first Irish entry for the Volvo Ocean Race immediately compelling and was reassured as other top Irish sailors were also being brought on board.

Justin Slattery, an old sailing mate from setting a round-the-world record on the giant catamaran *Cheyenne* was also an early recruit. Decades earlier, both of us had encountered *NCB Ireland* which had inspired us then. Reared in County Wexford but with his early sailing experience being in Cork, where he was born, Slattery had been the bowman for Mike Sanderson's winning *ABN AMRO* team in the previous Volvo Race and brought valuable insights from that campaign. Like me, he had also been waiting for a chance to sail for Ireland in a major ocean race and he brought an edge to the crew panel with his experience plus sheer, gritty determination, especially when under pressure such as sail changes in rough seas when the job calls for perseverance regardless of the conditions.

Ian 'Soapy' Moore's track record as an Irish navigator on the professional circuits for America's Cup teams as well as major offshore and long-distance races made him an ideal choice and a coup for the project in this critical role on board. He was a long-standing navigator with Walker and had sailed as navigator with *Team Illbruck*, the 2001–2002 Volvo Ocean Race winning 60-footer. And, being based on the Isle of Wight, he was already well known to many of the team members. His job on board was to soak up information both before the race and during it, to crunch numbers and run tactical software while all or most of the time cooped up in a dark and stuffy corner below decks, surrounded by electronic instruments. It was about as far removed from the popular image of yachting – sipping iced drinks on a palatial vessel in the company of glamorous people. And if ever he did find himself with spare time, there was plenty for him to do on deck or when needed if drama took over.

Also recruited were Dubliners Johnny Mordaunt and Johnny Smullen who would become the heart and soul of our shore team with their decades of experience in project management. James 'Jimbo' Carroll was the third Dub on the shore team and was the 'BC' or boat captain from the outset and we now had a distinctly Irish backbone to the team.

For all of us throughout our careers comprising years of competing on various teams for other countries, or for private individuals or sometimes multinational corporations the size of Ireland, such campaigns always left us longing for a chance that one day we might see the green, white and orange flying from our own Irish entry in a transglobal ocean race.

After we signed on together, both Slattery and I were often asked whether we would not have preferred the skipper's role. Surely an Irish entry demanded an Irish skipper? The question missed the point completely. It was not and never is about who gets to be the boss. It's about getting the job done and Walker was the right man for that job. Sea law requires a 'person-in-charge' to be ultimately responsible and our media and popular following also look to an individual as a figurehead. Yet, in a team situation, having an effective skipper is just one element of a result and taking a part share in that performance remains at the core of what drives each member of the crew. Being part of that was everything Slattery, Moore and I could have asked for when we signed up. That, plus lifting the trophy as overall winners, of course.

An economic build price from a branch of the Australian McConaghys boatbuilders in China was the beginning of the Sino-Irish link and when sponsorship from Shandong Lingong Construction Machinery linked to the Volvo corporation followed, *Green Dragon* took her name. Although an option to buy the winning boat from the last race existed, management knew that both crew and funding might not be available had they pursued this route.

We always knew it was going to be tight, launching a new design barely five months before the start. But the many positives and reassurances from team management that everything was on track left us to concentrate on boat and team preparations in the early summer of 2008. With only five months to go before the start of the race in which time we had to test sails, practise with the boat and train crew, our brand-new boat arrived on the deck of a ship after a five-week voyage. As the Volvo Open 70-footer was craned onto her dockside cradle in Portsmouth, the crate containing her underwater appendages was opened. Inside, the contents comprised the weighty, torpedo-like bulb that attaches to a long keel fin. This in turn attaches under the hull to the hydraulic rams inside the boat's hull that swing the whole arrangement to counterbalance the force of the rig and sails. This system is designed optimally to deliver the awesome speeds of these boats, yet as we pulled the last of the packing away, Slattery – who had won the previous Volvo Race on the first generation of these boats and already had a well-honed instinct for speed ingredients – needed to verify the keel weight, as both he and McDonald had warned of its importance to our performance. If it was underweight it would affect the overall ability of the boat to reach its best speeds.

It was a big day when boat and keel were joined together. All the elements had been built in different parts of the world – New Zealand, China, US and Italy – and all needed to fit perfectly and first time. Slattery and crew member Phil Harmer called over to the mobile-crane driver who was lifting the keel fin and bulb out of their packing cases. From the load sensors on the crane, he confirmed the weight. As the measurer took notes of the readings, he headed off to the office without telling anyone. Slattery's original concern was that in their enthusiasm at a new facility, the boatyard in China might have 'added in' construction materials and inadvertently pushed the weight of the boat over the optimum target. He had already wondered at the amount of internal structure that the previous race winner had not had – or needed. This latest generation boat should have been an evolution of this but instead appeared heavier. This concern was now added to a bigger issue. With a rule limit of 7.4 tonnes for the overall keel fin and bulb weight, the results of the weigh-in highlighted and made public for the all the team to see an ultimate flaw: the design specifications had placed some 600 kg in the fin, leaving the bulb light by over a half a ton. Keels, especially canting keels, generate the 'righting moment' that creates the power and speed potential of a sail boat. To be on target weight was crucial.

On that day, months before, when *Green Dragon* had not yet been sailed, Slattery returned home and apologised to his wife in advance for the frustration that inevitably lay ahead. As one of the best bowmen around, he carried a lot of credibility and, typically, he wasn't afraid to speak his mind and highlight our potential for underperformance. Our boat would struggle to match the other new builds in the fleet. Perhaps on the short in-port race courses the difference of half a knot in boat speed caused by our lack of power might not matter so much. But over the course of several days or even weeks, the difference would be massive and could translate into *Green Dragon* finishing days behind faster boats.

Yet Slattery remained completely committed to the project, purely because it was an Irish team and anyone with guts would not quit easily. We all felt the same; so too did McDonald, even though he had no Irish connection; we all decided to stick with the programme. Offers from other teams were made to some of us in the months leading up to the start but the programme was already up and running and our Irish team came first.

The Team

If an underweight keel was *Green Dragon*'s Achilles' heel, it was probably about as significant a problem that could have existed short perhaps, of the boat itself falling apart. But the heart of the issue went beyond the design of the appendage and all the way to the roots of the project, something that was far away from the minds of the sailing and shore crew.

In the months following her arrival into Portsmouth in June 2008, the issue of *Green Dragon*'s weight bubbled away in the background. It was not too late to remedy the situation and regain a competitive edge. A redesign of the keel and work on the hull to rebalance the all-up weight of *Green Dragon* could be managed within the remaining time before the start of the race in mid-October, or at worst we could receive a new keel fin in Cape Town. Twenty years previously, the *NCB Ireland* entry had cost IR£4 million to campaign. Fast forward to 2007 and the cost of building a state-of-the-art racing yacht stood at €4 million alone, without all the other costs of wages, expenses, sails, shore bases and new technologies that would require at least another €10 million to just scrape by with. But Walker's reality as skipper was a world removed from that of watch leader and the rest of the sailing team. What he knew and we did not was that the project simply did not have the financial cushion or the time to throw a handbrake turn into the programme and address the keel issue.

Together with Boag, Walker strategically brought forty people under the umbrella of the campaign, comprising all the elements of our racing team: experienced sailors, talented newcomers, technical expertise, logistics and applied resources.

Neal McDonald, arguably one of the best offshore sailors in the world, had competed in six round-the-world races including two as skipper in this event. We had raced together on a record circumnavigation attempt with Ellen MacArthur on *Kingfisher B&Q* in 2003. McDonald could be relied upon to take the wheel and steer accurately and fast in even the most demanding sea state for an entire watch without fatigue. His presence alone brought an air of gravitas and reassurance to the crew panel that lifted all of us. Crucially, he had offered the team his services before the boatbuilding started but the tight finances did not allow for this and his experience was lost at a critical phase.

Australian Anthony 'Youngster' Merrington joined *Green Dragon* with 120,000 ocean miles already logged through a campaign in the 2001–2002 Volvo Ocean Race on Team *SEB* and more recently with Paul Cayard on *Pirates of the Caribbean*. He had also sailed on the *Kingfisher B&Q* circumnavigation.

Race rules required each team to sail with three under-30-year-olds so up-and-coming talent was sourced for the team. Phil 'Wendy' Harmer had sailed in the previous race with the *ABN AMRO 2* youth team. He became responsible for all our sail inventory and maintenance and, after McDonald, he was the best helmsman on board, in part due to his experience on Australian 18-foot skiffs in Sydney Harbour.

Our only permanent Kiwi in the team, Andrew 'Animal' McClean was a big, strong easy-going bloke with a degree in mechanical engineering that would be invaluable, especially at sea, for the inevitable breakages. As he worked with Southern Spars in Auckland, he took responsibility for everything to do with our rig.

Freddie Shanks who sailed extensively with Walker in the MedCup TP52 inshore circuit joined Slattery on the bow. He held numerous youth titles as a former champion boxer and doubtless this discipline helped make him ultra-reliable with a steady dependability I came to appreciate as we shared the same watch at sea.

And all the time while the team was being drawn up, Australian Tom Braidwood was in China with his family. As a boatbuilder and project manager on behalf of the team, during the build Tommy got to know the boat intimately and made the crucial decisions for the deck layout and equipment that we would later come to reply upon so heavily. As he was already an experienced ocean racer, he was the ideal candidate to be the boat captain during racing phases and opposite number to Jimbo on the shore crew. His work ethic was akin to a whirlwind; he got stuck in and worked hard and was not slow to point out if others weren't pulling their weight: a true-blue Aussie who said things the way they were.

When the team secured sponsorship from the three Chinese companies, a funding crisis was averted, at least temporarily, and *Green Dragon* took her name to become co-flagged. The race required that an MCM – media crew member – be carried and be responsible for sending the constant stream of video, images, interviews and updates from the boat during the race. The role also included food preparation duties, though 'cook' would be a gross over-statement. The Chinese involvement required some representation in the crew line-up so Guo Chuan was recruited to sail as MCM.

He had started sailing in 1996 and was the first-ever Chinese participant in the single-handed mini-transatlantic class so he had previous experience from a demanding event. He was selected from trials with other Chinese sailors and his gentle manner belied his physical toughness and great stamina. Later, months after his selection, Guo earned the nickname 'the human cannonball' from an incident when *Green Dragon* was surfing through heavy seas at close to 100 per cent performance. He was crouched in the companionway filming the waves washing along the decks and partly submerging the crew huddled on deck. In the noise and the chaos of *Green Dragon* sailing on the edge between control and wipe-out, Nelly shouted through the crashing waves that even in the hatchway he needed to be clipped on. Nodding that he would obey but also persevering just a bit longer to finish his filming sequence, he started to retreat from the torrent of water sweeping aft along the deck past the shelter of the companionway and pilot house.

In an instant, the boat hit the back of a much larger wave ahead and in the next second, the boat, rig and all of the crew on deck shuddered from around 30 knots to a sudden halt. Instinctively, all on deck gripped a secure point tightly but our Chinese mate, who was just re-entering the hatch, was disoriented by the surprise boat movement and lost his grip, continuing his forward movement at full speed.

Slattery, resting off watch in his bunk inside, watched in amazement as our media man was propelled through mid-air, managing a complete back flip before finally touching down, head first into a bucket deep in the bilge of the boat. A minute later, he emerged, grinning sheepishly though bloodied from a cut forehead and murmuring 'I okay, I okay . . .'

Though times had changed from years past when Whitbread race entries carried a dedicated cook to deal with freezers full of real food, the role of MCM risks becoming a similarly thankless one – thankless because no matter how high the standard of cuisine, the worst food critic is a hungry sailor. As increasingly weight-dependent racing boats demand that luxuries such as fresh food be replaced by freeze-dried packets of monotonous meals that simply require reheating, beef stroganoff bears a striking resemblance to chicken and potatoes, which in turn seem to match the colour, taste and consistency of lamb curry. And desserts aren't much better, just sweeter, so suspicions run high that the recipes are variations on a theme.

But not all the freeze-dried manufacturers incur ill feeling and even differences between regional factories can be detected after months at sea. An American brand is one such supplier and the popularity of its USA products score higher than its UK counterparts amongst many ocean-racing crews. Preparation is a straightforward procedure: go to the daily food bag and select a meal from the array of identical packets pre-packed by the shore team. Cut the sachet open, pour into a large pot of water, soak thoroughly, heat and serve. Severely uncomfortable consequences await those failing to rehydrate fully a meal that can continue this process during the digestion process by soaking up vital body fluids and leading to stomach aches and constipation.

The MCM role could so easily have become a surrogate cook, even for these relatively simple meals. But although his duties included this and even mopping out the bilge in heavy weather, no other assistance was permitted in the racing of the boat in order to prevent teams simply inserting a top sailor into the role and boosting their on-board resources. Between these duties and the potential intrusiveness of his cameras that would appear in reality-TV-style awkward moments, Guo could have been an obvious person to be picked on as the butt of jokes for stressed crew, although this would have been too easy and unfair. However, as his English improved and he detected the subtleties of deck humour, he was soon well able to give as good as he got and share in the banter. On one occasion, when the food bowls were passed up on deck, it turned out that this particular batch of freeze-dried fare had not come from the preferred US factory but rather from its UK manufacturing operation. As the on-watch crew fed themselves, Nelly took his first few spoonfuls before delivering an unfavourable review.

'What the fuck is this?' growled McDonald. 'We can't eat it, it'll fucking kill us.' Guo heard the remark and appeared on deck.

'What's going on, Guo?' he snapped, albeit with a smile.

Everyone knew that although Guo had cooked the food, it wasn't his fault. There was brief pause and then, to everyone's delight, Guo delivered a perfect put-down.

'English-food, mate,' he replied. 'English food . . .'

Speechless but still smiling, Nelly withdrew while everyone else cheered 'Nice one, Guo!' for having managed the rare feat of getting one past Nelly.

Nevertheless, a separate week-long series of wind-ups between Guo and Slattery somehow kicked off and in the background a few of the other lads joined in for the *craic*. Personally, I would never think of taking on Slattery even for fun: when it comes to wind-ups and slagging, it doesn't take much to spark him off so it is not a road I care to go down. Sea boots started disappearing overboard and a rotting fish was discovered in a sleeping bag. Avoiding tension, even of the good-natured kind, had to be a priority so they finally called a truce.

Although permanent crew, the core of team members afloat still needed time off for family commitments so plans were included to swap in guest crew for various legs during the nine months of the race. Scotsman Ian 'Budgie' Budgeon was already well known to many of us and sailed for two legs. Wouter 'the router' Verbraak from the Netherlands managed to sail on three different boats during the race and he alternated with Steve Hayles, a race veteran from Southampton plus Jean-Luc Nélias from France as relief navigators for Soapy who took paternity leave at times from the boat. For in-port races, we were permitted to sail with additional crew so Kiwi Chris 'Maniac' Main was another stand-in.

Overall, whether permanent or stand-in, any crew member's prospects boiled down to not just being a good sailor with a useful skill or craft, but also to the subtle art of fitting in. In the case of ocean racing, this means knowing how a race boat operates and how to plug in to an established and tight-knit group of people. Creating an effective team means bringing together people with not just different skill sets, but different and compatible personalities. This is the harmony Walker sought from the outset and it was achieved despite the lack of financial resources. Simply put, money cannot buy relationships of any kind and this was true for the whole *Green Dragon* team.

Team Debrief in Cape Town, End of Leg I

Walker called the group together and the Cape Town meeting got under way. In the scheme of things, there was nothing especially unusual in such a crew meeting: ashore, they were a daily occurrence; while afloat, Walker would gather his navigator and both watch leaders into session at least once but sometimes three times daily to analyse tactical options, weather forecasts, fleet positions, boat manoeuvres and sail plans.

But a leg debrief is a different session. This meeting would be forensic in the hunt to extract improved performance from all departments on board: job lists, time lines, conclusions, future developments, how the boat is sailed and occasionally interpersonal issues (though it is important that the meeting does not get blocked by such problems and to limit the level of analysis to avoid 'bagging' individuals and concentrate on changing what can be changed).

All the routine issues such as the work-list of breakages and technical issues with the boat had already been emailed ashore during the leg so the boatbuilders and sailmakers were ready with solutions and fixes. These were still discussed under each heading – to get the easy stuff out of the way.

Less easy to fix were the unspoken problems, or rather, the problems that were spoken of but had been parked to avoid a breakdown of personal and working relationships in the close crew. In fact, in a less-gelled team, interpersonal disputes could easily have erupted on board, given the extended periods at sea in a constant state of competition. Crew compatibility is one constant that has defied the march of technology. But for Walker and his *Green Dragon* team, the single unspoken problem continued to be the one for which no solution existed and depending on when and whether each of us accepted its reality, it would remain unmentionable: because our keel was light and our boat was heavy, we would lack boat speed at critical times.

It could have been a production meeting for any corporation's business. Freshly showered and shaven, clean clothes – team uniforms – and fed with real food served to us on the dockside on arrival, there was a happy buzz in the room before the group was called to order. There was no need to belabour the details – we had all been present – so Walker briefly summed up the outcome of the past three weeks of relentless effort. In fact, it had ended up being more successful that most of us were prepared to acknowledge.

He began the meeting's reports following a careful agenda that reflected the on-board watch-keeping structure, picking through the details of our race thus far. The skipper and navigator operated as their own team with an ad hoc watch system at sea as they prepared the strategic options based on the latest weather data and fleet performance and positions. These objectives were then passed to the watch captains who, along with their crew on deck, agree how best to deliver our fastest speeds based on our sail inventory and likely weather in the coming hours. We would also review the latest 'skeds' or scheduled reports of the performances from the other seven boats in the race and these updates became a staple of our daily diet like the rise and fall of internationally traded stocks and bonds. And the graph hadn't been very encouraging, almost from the get-go.

The start from Alicante before tens of thousands of spectators both afloat and ashore had been marred for us by a problem with our hydraulic canting keel system, which slowed our manoeuvring and robbed us of the chance to scorch away from the start. But we managed to stay in touch with the leaders for the first few days until it became apparent that, even at this early stage, favourites were emerging within the eight-boat fleet. That we weren't leading the fleet did not surprise any of us on board *Green*

Dragon. As all eight boats reached the Strait of Gibraltar, we were not alone with technical problems – but all boats would expect teething issues of some kind, regardless of the amount of preparation involved.

As a procession southwestwards along the coast of Morocco formed, it was instantly clear that in these steady trade winds, tactical options to deliver an edge and get a jump on the leaders were severely limited. Walker and Soapy agonised: a risky 'flyer' was on the cards and a make-or-break gamble was called for ahead of the first scoring gate on the southern side of the equator, still almost ten days of hard racing away. A call was needed on whether to sail between the Canary Islands of Gran Canaria and Tenerife or to stay closer to the coast of Africa. The leaders opted for the latter and held their ground while our call involved dicing with the wind shadow from the steeper Canarian mountains. Result: marginal loss of miles but no nearer getting our break. It was never going to be a race-changing move but conventional race wisdom dictates the need to sail always in the same wind as your rivals.

The next tactical call arrived two days further south, on the approach to the Cape Verde Islands. But by now, a combination of our lack of boat speed was starting to show as we trailed the leaders by up to 100 nautical miles. Fleet leader *Ericsson 4* had to make a brief stop to drop off a sick crewman. The rest of the fleet was inadvertently duped by the medical emergency on board and covered *Ericsson 4* skipper Torben Grael, assuming his was the best strategy.

Further behind and with less to lose, Soapy made the bold but strategic call to break from the fleet and sail westwards. He had spotted a weather window of favourable winds and, looking ahead to the windless doldrums zone 60 miles north of the equator, reckoned we could make a fast transit of the area by heading deeper into the Atlantic Ocean. Statistically, the doldrums are easier to cross further west but it becomes a question of paying extra miles to get to the optimum crossing point. There was a spread of 50 to 90 miles between us in the west and the main fleet further east as we all dived southwards for the equator. It proved to be just the jump we needed and within three days, *Green Dragon* shot from third last on the water to a solid lead and first place which we held all the way into the southern hemisphere and the scoring gate at the Brazilian island of Fernando de Noronha, 200 miles off South America.

It was a great way to start the race and for a time we were tricked into thinking we were on a roll. There was a minor celebration on board as we picked up the first ocean-racing points on the first leg of a ten-month race. It was a good lift for the crew but raised false hopes and allowed some people to remain in denial and for the rest deferred the truth of our poor pace. We had picked up four points for first place and a valuable morale boost for a celebration that was short lived; even the younger crew as much as the veterans on board were all too aware of the long, long race ahead. Privately, we were all conscious of our Achilles' heel that had been revealed to us on that fateful day almost six months earlier when *Green Dragon* arrived from the boatbuilders' yard in China.

The race boiled down to accumulating points for high performances, whether at the end of the ocean stages or during each leg at scoring gates or closer to land in the in-port race series. But in spite of our navigator's genius, it is simply not possible to win on tactics alone in a ten-month race. There were intelligent sailors on every boat and hoping otherwise wasn't remotely realistic. All the other teams had good sailors and good navigators, and most had good boats going fast in the right direction.

Our boat's lack of keel weight would become even more apparent in reaching conditions – when the wind is blowing at right angles to the direction of the boat – and the fastest point of sailing when we should expect the best performance, such as the sprint across the South Atlantic Ocean to the finish of Leg 1 in Cape Town. However, from the moment we reached Fernando de Noronha, our tactical options were reduced to negotiating the weather of the St Helena or South Atlantic high-pressure system. Regardless of which way we headed for Cape Town, the freshening wind would quickly lead to fast reaching weather and our precious lead would evaporate.

American Ken Read on *Puma Ocean Racing* soon began duelling with *Ericsson 4*'s five-times Olympic medallist Grael and the pair sped away as winds gusted near gale force for almost a week and we were left in their wake. In turn, we started matching Grael's stable-mates on *Ericsson 3*, duelling between third and fourth places as a podium spot beckoned in Cape Town.

We began the dive towards South Africa by investing a few miles going south after Cabo Frio off Brazil, trying to position ourselves for the first frontal system that would begin the shuttle ride across the South Atlantic. However, those 6 miles translated into 50 later on when the front came through further north than predicted. Otherwise we might have stayed with the heavy weather and 'surfed' the front for longer, as we could have held station with the front as it sped across the open ocean. Still, the stage turned out to be the fastest bit of sailing in the whole race. In what is known as 'fire-hose sailing' *Green Dragon* hit speeds as fast as the boat ever sailed: 36, 37, 38 knots in bursts but consistently holding 30 knots and we managed to average 25 knots as we worked hard to find the optimal set-up with the rig.

But we also allowed *Ericsson 3* to fall in behind us and slightly to the north so they managed to ride the front longer than us as the *Dragon* was sailing more directly to Cape Town compared to their faster VMC sailing, a strategy which is best described as follows: when the route is free and you have no specific constraints, point the boat down the fastest angle and concentrate on the boat speed.

The helter-skelter ride also came with a hefty price on the crew. Although we managed to keep to the watch routine, kept driving hard and getting some rest, quite a few small injuries resulted from accelerating down waves and stopping at the bottom in a constant stop-start motion. Not everyone was lucky enough to stage Guo Chuan-style acrobatics. In one especially rough patch, Walker was crushed on the helm by three of the guys who were washed along the deck by a wave with tremendous force that would have swept all four overboard had it not been for their harnesses. In another swamping, I found my arm trapped under the traveller before it was extended backwards as the rush of water pushed me along the deck and strained my safety harness with huge force.

The decks were constantly awash and it was hard to see ahead even using helmets and visors. All agreed that more development was needed in the class to add protection on deck but minimising weight and windage were higher priorities for the designers in the quest for maximum boat speed. In these conditions, seamanship becomes paramount, knowing where the limits of boat and crew lie while still going fast. The reality was plain to see: under certain circumstances these boats can be sailed faster than the crew can physically control them and survive.

Three days out from Cape Town, we collided with a sunfish (though in hindsight, I think it was more likely to have been a whale). The boat came to a sudden sickening stop and everyone leapt to pull up the daggerboards or look through the hull window to see the keel and inspect for damage. A complete check was needed so we had to stop the boat, drop sails and send a man overboard for a closer look. Sometimes, such a check requires the keel to be canted but it wasn't needed this time: the keel fairing was clearly damaged, judging by the vibration and noise from the water rushing past.

While the fairing is sacrificial, sailing hard without it risks letting water into the keel system and this in turn could have knock-on effects. Sailing conservatively cost at least half a knot. Now to the south of us, *Ericsson 3* had drawn level and was getting through with apparent ease and soon we slipped to fourth place just days from South Africa. Still, a technical infringement saw *Ericsson 3* penalised in Leg 1 and we were awarded third place along with our first for the scoring-gate performance. But the result fooled nobody, least of all ourselves.

And as Walker finished summarising the leg at our debriefing meeting in Cape Town, it was clear that even though mistakes had been made across the fleet and that despite Soapy's brilliant tactical call that won the early part of the leg, errors in the fleet would not happen as often in future. After just 6,500 miles of racing, the writing was already on the wall for the *Green Dragon* and the challenge was only beginning. And although those of us who had accepted our handicap were adjusting to the prospects of not winning the race, talking up our prospects both in private and in public rang hollow.

◄○►

Round-table meetings were part of normal team life and we would have several in any one stopover. But the first leg debrief was inevitably quite intense as we were able to assess clearly the issues that were starting to appear, principally the boat-speed problem. What we didn't know was that Walker himself was not even certain that we could continue in the race as the money was not there to fund the team.

In spite of the clear difficulty, there were still denials and resistance to the notion that we weren't going to win the race, in an effort to boost morale. Positive winning attitude is the textbook approach to morale but an optimistic attitude that is not realistic does not produce results either, especially if there is an action that needs to be taken to solve a problem. Sometimes simply acknowledging that a particular problem exists will help solve it or lead to a path that will provide other solutions or perhaps just minimise the damage. It was key to acknowledge that the boat was slow. 'Let's not beat ourselves up about it' was the official line agreed amongst the group.

In the meantime, we watched the cut and thrust of the race that took place ashore, in the protest room, in heated debates over interpretations of racing and design rules. The technical infringement by *Ericsson 3* in the first leg was a saga that predated the start of the race, even before *Green Dragon* had completed its build. The *Ericsson* team had prepared in force for their second time entering the event, with two boats, two crews and an extensive design programme led by the designer of the previous race winner, Juan Kouyoumdjian. As a key part of the development programme, three keels had been built. But the 'design envelope' had been pushed too far and in the final months leading up to the race the team of naval architects rectified the problem under the close eye of the Racing Rules committee. By Alicante in the final weeks before the race, the keel was once again measured and to the surprise of the team was ruled non-compliant. Having been assigned to *Ericsson 3*, it would now be replaced with a new one in Cape Town, much to the frustration of the fully Scandinavian crew as they immediately received a points penalty before the race had even started.

Leg 2: Cape Town to Cochin, India

On the second leg, from Cape Town to Cochin on India's west coast, we were blasting through the Roaring Forties and into the Southern Ocean on an easterly heading and had progressively changed down from our big spinnaker to the small kite and from there to the fractional Code Zero headsail. As the wind turned squally and blew up to 40 knots, gale force, we reduced our sail area again by furling the headsail temporarily and sailing with full mainsail alone as we were starting to get sustained gusts of 50 knots.

With days remaining before our turn northwards, we were still surfing under this single sail but running the risk of transferring all the huge loads from the boat and rig to a possible weak point and, sure enough, a loud bang – the sound that we all dread – brought everyone quickly on deck. Our boom had done something that it shouldn't: it had snapped in two pieces and now swung around wildly, hanging from the clew of mainsail at one end and still attached to the mast at the other.

Nelly had been on the wheel, driving the boat hard and fast – one of the principal reasons that the *Green Dragon* did as well as she did at other times – and typically on this occasion, despite the break, he didn't let up and kept on driving as fast as the boat would allow. Everyone else, without panic or drama, swung into the roles that we had planned for just such an eventuality. Slattery coordinated the operation, starting with getting the boom off the mainsail. A job list was created and people formed into work groups based on their skill sets. Slattery wrestled the boom off the mainsail and onto the deck and the Code Zero was unfurled once more. Daylight helped and we did not stop racing, not for even a minute.

The repair strategy was to splice the boom back together using our emergency supply of carbon and epoxy resin but the location of the break, two-thirds of the distance from the mast, was certain to mean the boom would break again. A complicated system of ropes and pulleys was rigged so that we could control the mainsail off the back of the boat. It wouldn't give us anything like an optimal sail plan and our trimming ability would be severely hampered. Despite the limitations, we were still able to continue racing and grab third place at the scoring gate.

As we emerged from the Southern Ocean, we were holding our own, staying relatively close to the front of the fleet, as others dealt with their own problems, such as Ken Read on *Puma* who had the far more severe problem of the collapse of internal structural reinforcing stringers inside the hull. They had already reckoned their own keel was 20 kg underweight and that was causing them performance issues; this brought wry smiles to our faces. Elsewhere, both of the *Telefonica* team boats were discovering that their rudders were too small for the conditions and were in turn hampered. Bouwe Bekking's highly rated *Telefonica Blue* broke one of her two daggerboards. It would be fair to say that, as this was the second time rudder problems had occurred, they were unprepared for the race having spent most of the training period in the shelter of the Mediterranean. Only Grael on *Ericsson 4* seemed unaffected by the conditions.

It was a clear lesson that 80 per cent of the race is won before you get to the starting line and relies on a good boat, a good team, time and budget to make it happen. Even with all four elements, the trick in a big campaign is getting the balance right between spending and resources; the bigger the campaign, the harder the balance. As we crossed the equator for the second time, the fleet began to converge for a final sprint to the Cochin finishing line. Often, Soapy would appear on deck between his navigation schedules to help out, usually grinding, moving sails and sometimes steering. We all had a vague awareness of when a position report was due in to update us on the fleet's performance as we were sailing along. When these 'skeds' arrived, it was as if someone had a death in the family. The intercom on deck would crackle as Soapy announced in his Eeyore-like monotone the official reports that invariably showed us lagging further behind the faster front runners.

To counter the deflating effect of the skeds, we had an ongoing debate about whether the Volvo sked, which was a rhumb line (or direct route), was fairly useless compared to our own version, which took into account local conditions and the other boats' performances. Sailing in waters largely unknown to modern racing sailors, local wind effects were generally theoretical but Soapy once more appeared set to outmanoeuvre the fleet as we stayed to the west of the fleet in a better breeze. This time, even with our damaged boom handicapping our performance, Soapy was again digging us out from the back of the fleet and his call looked like holding all the way to the finishing line. We opted to use 'stealth mode' to hide our position from the fleet in the skeds for twenty-four hours but this time, however, his magic was not to be.

Bekking on *Telefonica Blue* managed to grab second-place honours for the leg. Both *Telefonica* boats got it right, more by accident than design, when another breakage forced them to ignore the routing advice to go east and they had sailed the direct route to India. *Puma* and *Delta Lloyd* were further behind but when the decision came to tack inshore, the breeze died and we were parked up, allowing the two boats behind us to get by. We were placed second last and felt aggrieved that the result did not reflect our effort of racing effectively without a boom over the 4,450 miles from South Africa, which included our third place at the Kerguelen Islands scoring gate. The park-up cost us a podium place and a fateful air of acceptance took over the team. Our pre-race goal, aside from winning, was to achieve a podium result by the end of the 39,000-mile course. Even this task appeared daunting when the smallest decision could have such crucial outcomes. Every battle would count, whether at sea or ashore. We would certainly be held to the rules by the other boats if we infringed and we planned to act likewise.

Ashore in Cochin, Walker decided to draft Jimbo on board as event fatigue was starting to affect the original crew members. Tommy had been working on the project non-stop, from the earliest days of the build straight through to delivery, fit out, race training and all the way to the start of the race in Alicante. It was vital to rotate key crew members and although it was always intended that this would be an option, the tight finances meant it had not been planned very well.

With no back-up sailors planned, Jimbo was an obvious choice for Walker, and he boosted the Irish quota on board. He was already popular with the crew and known as a very hard worker, methodical and as the boat captain from the shore team, he worked as opposite number to Tommy afloat. As the 'BC', he managed the job lists very effectively for the team.

His arrival on board as a sailing crew member also allowed him as a newcomer to witness first-hand the boat's shortcomings that we had been complaining about. Fitting seamlessly into the watch system, he was able to see the other boats pull away in conditions where we should – in theory at least – have been able to match them for boat speed. 'Jaysus, I knew there was a speed problem but I never realised it was *this* bad,' he declared after another set of skeds came in.

Leg 3: Cochin to Singapore; Leg 4: Singapore to Qingdao, China; Leg 5: Qingdao to Rio de Janeiro

When *Ericsson 3* started the third leg from India to Singapore a basic error was made by them in not respecting the limit mark South of Sri Lanka. We pushed hard for the race office to have our protest heard and a penalty applied to the Swedes.

Leg 4 proved to be a true test of the Volvo fleet, upwind against the prevailing monsoon for 2,500 miles to Qingdao in China. *Ericsson 3* was amongst a clutch of boats to develop structural problems following storm force winds in the South China Sea. I was on a break from racing for this leg but could watch the unfolding storm online. To Bekking's eternal credit, which earned him the respect of the fleet, *Telefonica Blue* managed to continue racing in the storm force winds while Grael on *Ericsson 4* sought shelter and anchored close to the Philippines.

Green Dragon was now fighting for fifth place in the race directly against *Ericsson 3*. Although she broke some carbon bulkheads and also sought shelter off lush beaches near Manila, the Scandinavians had much worse damage as their bow section began to delaminate. As just four boats, including *Green Dragon,* pressed on to China, *Ericsson 3*'s skipper, Magnus Olsson, opted to pull into Taiwan for repairs. In fact, the repairs involved milling an entirely new section of hull in Italy, flying it and a boatbuilding team to Taiwan where the repair was completed, including a new paint job. Their crew was rested and, due to the delay, the team missed the in-port race in China. Qingdao was a quieter place due to the storm-depleted fleet though the presence of Guo managed to generate a massive following for *Green Dragon* in China so a non-event was avoided.

Yet Olsson did not just miss the in-port race in Qingdao. After the repairs were complete, *Ericsson 3* only arrived in China the night after the *next* leg had started out from Qingdao to Brazil and fresh crew boarded their boat with new sails and supplies in record time. *Ericsson 3* also collected points for the previous leg and were soon back into the thick of the leg to South America, a mammoth 12,000-mile leg. After examining the rules and consulting with the *Puma* team with a view to making a joint protest against what we regarded as an unfair advantage, we found nothing in the rules that was directly contravened and the race went on. Ultimately, *Ericsson 3* did a fantastic job of first turning the boat around in a couple of hours and then sailing out less than a day behind to deliver an incredible result of first place for the leg.

Throughout the race and especially heading to Rio de Janeiro, we were our toughest taskmasters, quietly ignoring the fact that four of the eight boats had not completed the course with the rest of the fleet: neither *Telefonica Black* nor *Team Delta Lloyd* had reached China and were instead shipped onwards after extensive repairs and refits. *Team Russia* also withdrew from the event in Singapore after Leg 3 when sponsorship funds ran out. And we considered *Ericsson 3* to have only partially sailed the full course but the tremendous result in the leg to Brazil vastly outweighed this fact. If the race had been tough on us since the heady days of the first leg into Cape Town, time did not bring an improvement and the depleted fleet only magnified the second last place we scored into Rio de Janeiro at the end of the gruelling stage from China.

Despite the carnival city's attractions, our Brazilian sojourn was marred by another low point in the campaign. Finances were at a crisis point and simply to complete the course would mean abandoning our sail replacement programme and taking a 50 per cent pay cut. The shore crew would be slimmed progressively and refits limited to essentials only. Our team physio had become a casualty even before leaving Alicante and now many of the shore crew would not even be present in Ireland, far less the end of the race. A senior member of the project management flew out to Rio to break the news to us. A small meeting was convened between him and the watch captains and shore managers.

'You'll probably think I'm a complete bollocks for doing this,' he said. 'We want you to take a 50 per cent wage cut for the rest of the race plus the month you've just worked.'

This was the month in which we had sailed through the Southern Ocean and around Cape Horn. We were now a long way from the project we had been promised. Breaking his habit of non-confrontation in such situations, Nelly responded.

'Yes,' he said. 'You are.'

It was no secret that some of the project backers misunderstood the professional nature of modern sailing. For some, the world hadn't changed since the first Irish Whitbread race entry when cheap deals and contra arrangements in lieu of payment were sometimes the norm. But a recession was looming and it was crunch time between professional sport and economics. Walker and Boag called a meeting of the whole project team, sailors and shore crew together. Sponsorship income from China was €500,000 less than agreed and while everyone was needed, even with the pay cuts and cost trimming the team would have to downsize. The situation was difficult to accept for all involved, on all sides.

And we lost Tommy Braidwood, too. Having returned to Australia for a leg-break, the travel allowance each of us had for family visits had not taken into account the extended distance he needed and the monies to bring him back to the boat had run out. We never saw him again but we shared his hurt and disappointment at not seeing his project completed. Yet we all stayed on; the team that Walker built didn't fall apart, though it did have an uphill battle ahead.

Leg 6: Rio de Janeiro to Boston

From Rio, the leg to Boston was pretty brutal despite sailing through the tropics and past the glorious sailing grounds of the Caribbean. We were now clearly lacking between 1 and

2 knots of boat speed against the nearest boats in matching conditions with matching sails, and Soapy had left us to return home for the birth of his baby daughter. Jimbo's first time crossing the equator and the traditional visit from King Neptune and Queen Codfish (Nelly and Slattery) was a temporary distraction from the fleet opening up ground on us.

The gap got bigger pretty quickly and every sked, every two hours, the report would invariably arrive: 'lost a mile . . . lost two miles . . . lost half a mile . . . gained a mile, back down again . . .' until eventually we were not sailing in matching conditions. It was simply a result of straight-line strategy: the fastest route to Boston was the most direct and no weather or alternative route would allow a passing lane.

As we trudged our way towards Boston at the back of the fleet, morale on board was as low as it could get.

To lighten the mood during the long hours sitting on the stack of sails, someone brought up the subject of alternative competitions that we might have a better chance at as traditionally there are often unofficial shoreside activities during the stopovers such as a football game or karting. The list started out with a burrito-eating contest and when someone mentioned table tennis and badminton, they had obviously missed the point. We needed a competition, something with no holds barred, boxing or wrestling or . . . ice hockey; now there's a sport: you don't like the look of the other guy, belt him over the head and then get your mates involved. So that was it: an inter-team ice hockey contest was the solution. Of course none of us could skate, but that didn't seem to matter. Surely all that's needed for a game like that is a bit of anger, a good hockey stick and some formidable opponents? The fact that amongst the other American and Scandinavian teams there were guys who could not only skate but were real players, did not deter our banter.

Big Thomas Johanson, the Finnish watch captain from *Ericsson 3*, a former Laser World Champion and Olympic gold medallist had been a semi-pro and would be a likely contender. *Puma* skipper Ken Read had a reputation on the rink and his bowman Jerry Kirby's standing as a giant on the ice was well known. As the fifty-year-old bowman on *Puma*, Kirby is a legendary figure. Hailing from Newport, Rhode Island, he has spent a career working the bow of the best boats in the world, with enormous enthusiasm and a generous nature that matches his size and formidable strength. The Claiborne Pell Bridge that spans the East Passage to Rhode Island has a 200-foot clearance and was a regular commute for Kirby to get to sailing. As legend relates, Kirby was already late for racing one day and had spotted his boat motoring down the river. He threw his sailing bag down from the roadway and then jumped off to land close to the boat where he was collected in time to go racing.

As our discussion turned from planning an ice hockey match to relating stories of various well-known sailors, the tension eased. But the frustration remained just beneath the surface until we finally finished the leg in Boston and we were unloading the mainsail. Eight crew members hoisted the weighty sail onto their shoulders and carried it up the dock in a dark mood. The dock security guard was clearing a path through the crowd that the lead crewman could see but the rest of us could not; we impatiently pushed ahead and past the guard, who rightly took offence. A complaint was made to the race office, which demanded an explanation from the team and we duly apologised for the incident.

At least Boston offered something to cheer us as the huge Irish interest there placed us as the firm local favourite, even upstaging Read and the boys on *Puma* who had already adopted the city as their home port and taken a hit song by the Dropkick Murphys as the boat's anthem. Slattery earned himself a rap on the knuckles for admitting in a media interview that our boat was 1.5 to 2 knots slow. His response was: 'What do you want me to do, lie about it?'

A sense that *Green Dragon* was coming home started to grow on the team; the pressure was back on and even though many of the team's sponsor expectations had already been met, ours certainly hadn't. Whatever about achieving a top three overall place in the race, we had yet to finish in the top three in any of the previous six legs and the transatlantic stage would effectively complete the circumnavigation. It was all over bar the shouting and Grael's *Ericsson 4* could sink and still win the Fighting Finish trophy. We badly needed a break; something to restore our confidence and morale.

And then Soapy returned.

Leg 7: Boston to Galway

It wasn't the most impressive of departures, really. Before a 'home' crowd and selected as first to dock out from Fan Pier in Boston, *Green Dragon* awaited her familiar team song,

'Elevation' by U2. If we could have taken an elevator we would have. Instead of Bono and The Edge, we were blasted by Mundy and Sharon Shannon with 'Galway Girl', apparently our new anthem in honour of our home port that we were about to sail for. But nobody had told the crew.

As the music blared and the thousands of spectators cheered, none of us was in his place for the well-rehearsed drill that involved juggling dock lines, mooring buoys and the team tender to ease the 70 feet of racing machine out of the tight confines of the dock. The din drowned out the calls forward as Guy Swindells, the race MC bade farewell to *Green Dragon*. Except that the mooring lines were still made fast. The *Dragon* bounced back and forth once or twice until the bowlines could be released but the fresh breeze had already caught us and it was not until our team rigid inflatable boat (RIB) with its twin 225 hp outboard engines roared up alongside and took a line to tow us that we could make good our escape and hide our blushes. It took us two minutes, three at the most, to leave the harbour and was the last thing we needed, although it only added to our resolve to get a good result into Galway. Our boat-handling skills were in full view and we hadn't even got a sail up.

<o>

From the earliest days of planning the campaign, we had expected that the transatlantic leg would suit us, being mostly dead downwind when stability would be less of an issue. There were also a few more tactical options, plus

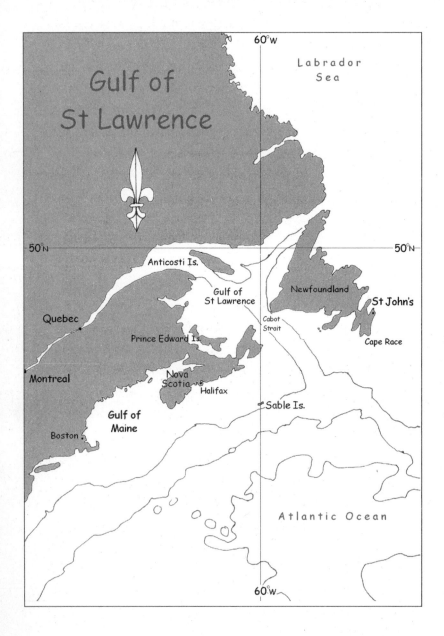

weather and current factors too; but that was before the race and now, as the underdog's underdog, we were in a place none of us had ever anticipated. Despite our setbacks, we still retained a bloody good crew, as good as any other and well able to sail fast in the tough conditions. Boston had been good to us. It had been friendly, safe and featured a good in-port race in front of the cityscape for the sponsors. But we were more than ready to get stuck into getting away from the USA and taking on the might of the Atlantic Ocean.

We had managed to pick up another sponsor in a deal facilitated by Volvo and now our transom sported the logo of Bwin, the online sports betting company that also sponsors Real Madrid – we were in good company for sure. That deal allowed the 200,000 followers of the race Internet game to choose tactical options for us for the leg that would be a small burden for Soapy and Walker but an interesting innovation for improving sailing participation. The leg also featured a whale protection zone plus ice exclusion zones in the early stages.

Incredibly, we managed to win the start right in front of the Boston waterfront and led the fleet away, though thick fog descended and spoiled the view for the spectators. For the first night and day, the cold fog stayed with us as we raced north, in constant touch with the front of the pack as we battled wind shear that stopped any of us getting into our stride. As we made for Cape Race at the edge of Newfoundland, we turned eastwards to skirt the ice zone where satellite imagery had warned that melting icebergs were further south than normal.

We now had to play the remains of the cold Labrador Current as it flowed southwards and then try and pick out where we might hitch our ride on the warmer Gulf Stream that was headed in our direction. We were also in the prime fishing grounds of the Grand Banks, *Perfect Storm* territory but thankfully outside hurricane season. Nevertheless, along with most of the fleet, we managed to snag our leeward daggerboard in a crab-pot marker that sawed into the carbon and dragged the boat almost to a halt. By the time we stopped, backed the mainsail so we could reverse up and cut ourselves free, we had lost ground. A short debate followed and we opted for a quick fix that would hopefully last us to Galway.

After five days, we cleared the eastern limit of the ice exclusion zone and were into the North Atlantic. The breeze was building and we were now sailing fast dead downwind with just a week remaining to reach the final approach to home. Swapping for first and second place with *Ericsson 4*, nobody dared to hope that we might get into Galway in first place: it was too early, too tempting to think ahead so we just had to take one day at a time. We were blasting through the ocean, continually filling and draining the cockpit as we ploughed through the cresting seas. We were in the same patch of the Atlantic where Hans Horrevoets was washed overboard from *ABN AMRO 2* in the middle of the night during the previous Volvo Ocean Race. The crew had managed the impressive feat of dropping sail, turning and retracing their path to recover him in less than twenty-five minutes. But he had already died and his memory lived with all the crews barely three years on. Yet we still thrilled in the conditions, living what he too had loved, an experience that rarely fails to get crews smiling despite the risk and soaking from the incessant spray, the on-deck crew continuously underwater as we pushed the boat harder than ever. We were producing some of the most exciting on-board footage of the entire race and the satellite feed of life on board was being broadcast daily into living rooms around the world as we neared Ireland. Slattery, underwater on the foredeck, produced his classic 'this is a prick of a job,' comment, and everyone at home believed him; no one had seen this side of ocean racing before.

Three days out from Galway, to our surprise we spotted another sailing boat crossing our path. It was sailing north and appeared to be heading for Greenland! In the dim light of dusk, we were able to make out that it was *Telefonica Blue*. By morning, it was clear they had delayed their gybe two hours longer and had overstood: we were now 50 miles ahead. Gradually, the wind came from behind onto our beam and righting moment became an issue once again. Grael started to edge ahead gradually. Worse still, the fleet was coming up from behind and Read and the *Puma* gang were gaining on us. Approaching the Aran Islands, the drag race started again and Read reeled us in and passed on by – third place would be a battle once again. Darkness fell for our final night at sea; we could see bonfires high up on the hill on Inis Mór, part of a chain of beacons lit specially to welcome the race to Galway.

Galway

Two boats ahead, three boats behind and approaching the coast at night in a dying breeze was a complete contrast to the previous five days of deep ocean racing in big seas. As we crossed into Galway Bay, we now knew we were in third place but still felt huge pressure – having to sail into a bay in the middle of the night with a failing breeze meant we could easily park up and lose again. We banked our hopes that the size of Galway Bay would mean some wind, enough to reach the finish.

Out of the darkness, a RIB pulled up beside us, her crew dressed for offshore conditions and all cheering madly. Nice welcome, we thought. But as we crossed the bay, the fleet around us grew and by the time we were close to the port where the channel narrows, the fleet was huge: you could have literally walked from one boat to another and in the middle of the night. And we were still trying to race.

With a full mainsail and spinnaker, going up a channel with zero room to bear away and drop sails was too risky so Walker called for everything bar the main to be dropped and we slowed to a crawl; we wouldn't be passed out now. Few of us had ever seen anything like this flotilla of well-wishers before, except perhaps for some race starts, but never in the middle of the night.

As we crossed the line, the mood on board was already very happy: we were finally on the podium with a third place for an offshore leg of the race, arguably one of the most dangerous and, most importantly, it was our homecoming. Job done.

We had no time to relax and celebrate as we still had our routine to maintain: drop the main, pack and stack the sails, get the scrutineers on board, unseal the prop shaft and prepare to simply walk off the boat on arrival. We were in automatic mode, dreamlike almost. In the space of an hour, we had been alone at sea with just a few other boats scattered around us for competition; now we were surrounded by hundreds of people cheering *us*, the *Green Dragon* team.

In the throng, I was amazed to spot another RIB packed with friends from Derrynane who had made the sea journey to be there. Our team RIB pulled up, crowded with the last of our shore crew and we were all together to share the result that was very nearly as good as a win: we had sailed a very solid race and put boats behind us.

A cooler appeared on deck, filled with some chilled beers that Johnny Mordaunt of our shore team had packed, a long-established tradition that flouted race rules banning alcohol for official occasions on board. Provided we didn't appear on camera, we would probably not incur the wrath of the race office but we were already far from caring. Still we had no idea what was about to happen. As the parade crept slowly towards Galway docks, we began to sense the noise and light coming from the inner harbour. I was standing in the cockpit but Slattery was on the bow and Soapy was at the mast so both could see what the rest of us couldn't yet view.

'Er, we've got a bit on here, fellas,' called Soapy, his face breaking into a grin as the sight of the enormous crowd lining every spare bit of space on the docks opened up to us and we could see the sheer scale of 9,000 people gathered at three o'clock in the morning. We never expected *this*.

By now, Jimbo was at the wheel as boat captain. There were the odd mutterings of 'No pressure, Jimbo . . .' – this wouldn't be the best moment to bump the dock – but most of us were by now completely enthralled by the welcome and indescribable feeling. Soapy was lepping around the deck, rejoicing and punching the air for this more-than-deserved victory. People we didn't know were calling out our names.

Jim Slattery arrived onto the dock with eleven pints of Guinness on a tray followed by Maurice Keller from Good Food Ireland, our Tourism Ireland friends who had kept us fed on arrival and promoted the country's artisan food producers, wowing our race friends around the world.

It was the moment that we could at last relax. Suzy-Ann on the dock, smiling with tears in her eyes, passed our eighteen-month-old son Oisín up to me for a hug while his little buddy James was with his dad, Nelly, who was grinning from ear to ear. Suddenly, everything felt worthwhile.

It was huge recompense and in the following days allowed us to walk around with heads held higher. The other crews were thrilled for us and the compliments flowed about the stopover and how their families had toured the west of Ireland and played golf. Laundries refused to charge for servicing the teams, locals warmly greeted the skippers by name on the street, every taxi driver in Galway knew about the race; crews had de facto freedom of the City of the Tribes.

The stopover and the *Green Dragon* podium place changed the outcome of campaign. Without it, the project would have been a failure. Nobody expected it to be as successful as it was, even though the Irish guys always knew that Galway as a colourful, traditional festival town would put on a good show. But it was more than just the usual stage-managed civic welcome – this had passion. What was special was that everyone got involved and, with an Irish team, felt able to overcome the worsening national economic situation and follow on from the recent Irish Grand Slam rugby success. Torben Grael provided the biggest surprise in that he did not return home at the end of the leg as usual. The Irish connected with the Brazilian, it seemed, and the local Brazilian community threw a house party for him. In fact, all seven skippers attended all the civic functions in Galway, a first in the race and a sign of huge respect and not something seen very often in professional sailing internationally. In other professional sports such as football, ninety minutes before a crowd of tens of thousands is a weekly occurrence and normal. But in sailing, which happens mostly out at sea, moments such as these occur – maybe – once every ten years. This was the emotion that kept the moment going even with the team on half-wages, kept the guys hanging on.

Leg 8: Galway to Marstrand, Sweden; Leg 9 Marstrand to Stockholm, Sweden; Final Leg 10: Stockholm to St Petersburg, Russia

With new life breathed into the team we carried on from Galway for the remaining three legs even though the race had already been won. The *Dragon* lead the fleet – again – out from our home port and down the west coast of Ireland in thrilling, windy conditions as the race hinged on running angles once more and suited us. Although we were already 'over-range' with our spinnaker, we watched *Ericsson 4* wipe out while trying to take our lead as they gybed. When we took our turn at the same manoeuvre, thanks to Nelly, we pulled it off, gybing smoothly as the wind reached gale force. We were punching well above our weight as we rushed past Derrynane where the lads had to endure my reminders that we were off 'God's country' and we held our lead past the towering Skelligs pinnacles and all the way to the Fastnet Rock.

Soapy worked his magic in the English Channel – home turf for him and Walker – and once again, we were all set for another nice result going into Marstrand, only to be passed again by Grael and Read on the final reach in so our podium ambitions were rounded off by our second third place of the race.

And while it could have been so much more, the lessons were hard learned. Grael and the *Ericsson* Racing Team were the hands-down winners from sheer firepower of budget, proper research and design, time on the water and pure talent. But given half a chance, with the same skipper, crew and shore team there isn't one of us who wouldn't want a second try to finish the job we set out to do. It may well be another twenty years before Ireland has another competitive entry in the round-the-world race but hopefully that crew will include a few of the 15,000 Irish school-children who came to visit us in Galway and followed us around the world.

Our project had come to an end. Our team would split finally and go our separate ways until the next opportunity. For Walker and Boag, this meant a fully funded entry for the next Volvo Ocean Race sponsored by the Abu Dhabi tourism authority in the United Arab Emirates and they drew Slattery to their ranks. Nelly was snapped up by the Spanish *Telefonica* team and Animal was selected for Team New Zealand's *Camper* entry. For me, this would be an invitation from Franck Cammas to join his *Groupama* sailing team in France to pull together an entry. Phil Harmer joined our programme a few months later.

Before long, we would all be at sea again and each would have another chance at winning this holy grail of ocean racing. But before I began the months of preparations again there were more important things to think about. Shortly after the *Green Dragon*'s campaign ended a new addition to the family was welcomed. Suzy-Ann gave birth to the most beautiful little girl in the world: Oisín now had a baby sister whom we named Neave.

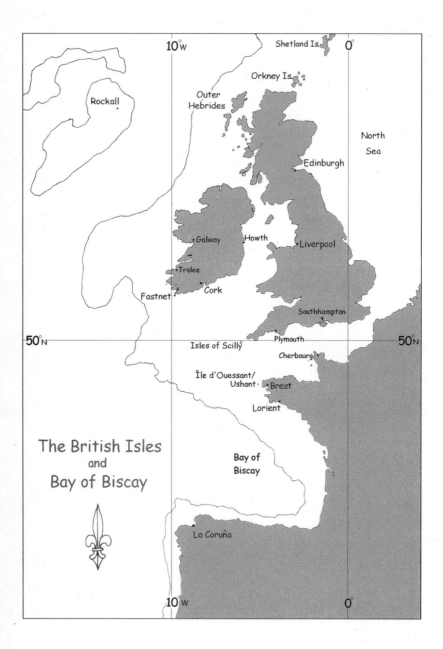

The British Isles
and
Bay of Biscay

2

Coming to Ireland

Incessant. Well, almost unceasing, but for brief respites in weather patterns. Steep, white-crested waves, grey-faced under blackened skies, swept eastwards across the North Atlantic and relentlessly driven by the wind, are the hallmarks of the long winter months for those living along Europe's westernmost seaboard.

Standing guard at the edge of the Atlantic at the south-westernmost edge of Ireland is the county of Kerry. Shaped by glaciers to become a formidable landfall and a brace against the onslaught of the ocean, the great peninsulas of Dingle, Iveargh and Beara, each flanked by once mighty rivers more than 400 million years ago are weathered more gently now, by wind, rain and sea. Summer transforms the region to near-paradise status as the temperature rises modestly and skies clear for the sun to light the natural beauty of the mountains, bogs and coast. The middle of these three capes is home to one of the best tourist attractions of any visit to Ireland; the famed Ring of Kerry rarely fails to impress even the most seasoned traveller. Winding out from the picturesque town of Killarney with its great Lakes and National Park, a country road takes in Kilorglin, Cahersiveen, Valentia Island, Waterville, Ballinskelligs, Caherdaniel and Sneem before ending up in Kenmare after a breathtaking tour de force.

Sometimes, visitors to the region on strict timetables simply speed through just the highlights of the route and so can miss out on some of the more subtle features that are revealed to more patient observers. Others opt to spend entire vacations in the area, soaking up the beauty of the landscape and the culture and rarely leave without resolving to return before too long. And some choose to make Kerry their permanent home.

Nature, even with the extremes of weather, was the priority for my parents, Roger and Susan Foxall, in 1968, in search of a fresh beginning and a place to raise a family beside the sea, close to mountains and amongst like-minded people who could see beauty even in nature's darkest forces.

It was summertime as their courtship turned towards marriage at the end of their student years on the banks of the Firth of Forth in Edinburgh where they met at a local sailing club. While The Beatles were rocking the Merseyside and far beyond, my parents were more occupied with enjoying sailing and the outdoors.

Mum's family came from Cheshire and lived on the Wirral Peninsula where my grandfather Frank was a fanatical small boat sailor. In his traditional Star class daysailer, a clinker-built wooden boat with a Gunter rig and centreboard, he won hundreds of inshore racing trophies, many of which he had previously bestowed. His enthusiasm for the sport was infectious and though my grandmother did not share his passion for sailing, from the age that she could walk, Susan 'crewed' on board, though was in reality more a form of movable ballast, at least in her early years.

Frank's love of life and affection for others revolved around a daily Guinness at West Kirby Sailing Club where Dad later became involved, standing in for his father-in-law-to-be on occasion to sail with Susan. With the tidal nature of the moorings, crews had to walk to the boats in advance of the flood and await the incoming waters. Despite the wait, it was occasionally noted by others that their sails were often down when they ought to have been up, whilst waiting on the mooring.

But for my Dad, pursuing his passion for sailing answered a calling within his family that spanned several generations though he deliberately avoided a full-time career at sea. Uniquely, being so distant from the sea, midlands people have a special fascination and a calling to the sea. Though living on the east coast at Eastbourne, Roger's father, Gerald, and his family hailed from the Black Country but his ambition to go to sea for a career was thwarted by parental disapproval so he became an engineer instead and later took up teaching. Similarly, Roger's mother's family was from East Anglia and their interest in matters maritime was more concerned with avoiding being flooded, as their home at Lowestoft was at the junction of the sea and inland waterways.

Even when Gerald and Barbara's first great adventure on the high seas came about – their honeymoon – the Second World War interrupted and their holiday on Sark was spoiled when the German invasion of the Channel Islands obliged them to make a short passage by paddle steamer to the Isle of Wight instead. Still, later in life they managed to cruise the Scottish islands together and this was also where Roger had his first taste of offshore sailing in a Shetland clinker-built double-ender from Tobermory in Mull to the Outer Hebrides during his time there as a postgraduate student. Dad's taste for sailing really took off through the good offices of the Scottish Council for Physical Education who acted as crew agents for owners of sailing boats.

At the start of Mum and Dad's relationship in 1967 they knew it was an instant fit and marriage was soon in the offing. They were certain that they wanted a healthy, outdoor lifestyle that combined their mutual interests in the sea and nature but a lack of funds was a significant obstacle. Both were before their time in choosing ecologically sound, sustainable values that might be seen as the norm from a modern perspective. They took an atlas and with a preference for either Scotland's Western Isles or Ireland, blindfolded they put a drawing pin into the map, resolving to make that place their first choice.

The pin stuck into the Dingle Peninsula at Derrymore Strand, 5 miles from the town of Tralee and the beating heart of County Kerry and within a short distance of the most westerly point of Europe.

By a stroke of good fortune, Dad secured a position as a contract architect in a local private practice and the move to Ireland began, prior to their wedding in 1968. His first project was a new guesthouse in Listowel. Much later, the Tralee Courthouse was falling down with dry rot until a visit from the Minister for Justice, who demanded it be restored, and so it became one of Dad's first larger-scale projects. He had visited Ireland as a student – the Aran Islands in Galway Bay – where the islanders wore traditional clothing, spoke in a different language and followed their unique lifestyle, which made culture shock less of an issue for him than it was at first for Mum.

Nevertheless, on arrival in Kerry, it was soon made known to him that not only would premarital cohabitation be frowned upon locally, even separate accommodation in the same town might be a source of angst and reflect poorly on the newly arrived professional – and his practice. During the first six months of their marriage, Dad commuted by ferry to visit Mum in England every month before she moved to Ireland and they lived in a flat above a shop in the town. With no money apart from a small loan from their best man, they looked for ways to supplement their income. Their first initiative was the curing of sheepskins that could be sold on to visiting tourists. They were friendly with the Tarants who owned a petrol station and from their shop they sold the Foxalls' produce. There was also a brief spell making costume jewellery and after a move further down the Dingle Peninsula, they ran tea rooms.

As an English couple, they made friends easily and though the Troubles in Northern Ireland were worsening by the week, they received as courteous and friendly a welcome as any respectful newcomers could ask for. Even a single exception to this, a minor verbal altercation between Dad and a builder on a site, saw the contractor return the following day with a fulsome apology and a bottle of Paddy whiskey at Christmas. They soon learnt that Irish people were ready to accept you as you are, not as you might be.

They moved to a rented small country cottage, prone to flooding in the winter and managed a deal with the owner who installed electricity for an extra £1 per week. Shortly afterwards, they discovered woodworm in all the furniture that came with the property and promptly brought it outside and burned it in a large bonfire. The owner arrived in the middle of the disposal and, instead of challenging them, quietly accepted their word that his property was beyond salvage and went on his way.

Another friend and neighbour who kept stables 'loaned' them a horse as they had a large field attached to the cottage. He then reckoned the first horse should have company and so lent them a second. After a few weeks, he arrived with a third horse 'in case the second got lonely while the first was out riding . . .' and the penny dropped that he might have been having overcrowding issues at his own stables; there was clearly more than one way to do business in Ireland.

Around this time, Tralee Bay Sailing Club at nearby Fenit Harbour was emerging as a bustling hive of recently founded club activity. Dad was introduced and sailed on various offshore races including to the Aran Islands and back, all along the exposed and rugged west coast. Len Breewood was a Scottish naval architect working for a German company and introduced Dad to Captain Eric

Healy, master of the Irish sail-training vessel *Asgard*, Erskine Childers' original gun-running yacht, and they became friends as he sailed regularly on board and became a watch leader. He later sailed on the *Creidne*, a temporary vessel when *Asgard* was ignominiously laid up in Kilmainham, and eventually joined Healy for voyages on the brigantine *Asgard II*.

Dad and Mum lived happily in their small cottage and, in 1969, I was born at a maternity hospital just across the Kerry border in County Limerick. Within two years, my brother Rupert was born and a more permanent home was needed for the larger family so they built a house overlooking the bay across to Fenit and under the 'shelter' of Slieve Mish mountain at Camp, 7 miles from Tralee, close to where the drawing pin first struck the map.

It was to become a salutary lesson in the realities of life on the exposed western seaboard. Dad quickly realised his mistake of building on a north-facing hillside on Dingle Peninsula. Despite the beautiful view over Tralee Bay, they lacked significant sunlight in winter. Aside from that, the site was fully exposed to northerly wind and seemingly non-stop sleet and hail. His mind was finally and quickly made up one winter night. As winds howled to hurricane strength, making the roof shake and causing the front gates to crash about wildly, threatening to break from their hinges, he resolved to begin a hunt for a new home.

After touring around various sites, many owned by farmers keen to sell up, the Foxalls and their two young children were brought to see a run-down house and smallholding at Bunavalla, overlooking Derrynane Harbour and close to the village of Caherdaniel on the south side of the Iveargh Peninsula. Mouldy bread decorated the old kitchen table but a pile of old tan sails in the corner, a link to the previous family's life on the outlying Scariff Island, caught Dad's eye and reminded him of the proximity to the water. Mum loved it immediately, for its location and garden that stretched down to the sea and Derrynane Harbour, and for its views over to the islands and out to the west.

Soon after moving to Bunavalla in 1978, Dan Gleeson at Castlecove was commissioned to build a 15-foot punt of larch on oak that would serve as a tender to be moored of the rocks the bottom of the farm. As Dad needed the car for his weekly commute to Tralee, Mum kept her bicycle on the other side of the harbour and would cross by boat before making her way for supplies from the small shop, nestled between two pubs, a church and a primary school in the local village, Caherdaniel.

At the weekend, Dad would make the two-hour 60-mile trip from Tralee via the supermarket in the bigger town to get the main supplies for the family. The arrangement of living half house, half caravan continued for two years as we slept in the latter and bathed in an old metal bath in front of the fire in the former. During this time our smallholding developed with haymaking, geese and hens, as well as cattle which Rupert and I learnt to milk. We could also get food from the sea so the punt came into its own for long-lining, feathering for mackerel and netting for bottom fish.

The hardship of separation during the week, enforced by a two-hour commute to and from Tralee on Monday and

Fridays for Dad, was easily matched by Mum's task of raising her two sons alone. But the support of neighbours in the surrounding townland on the slopes of Bunavalla could be relied upon to help out whether by childminding, friendship or, when needed, the occasional chastisement for the kids. The warmth of the valley community was a privilege that for my parents confirmed their final choice of home.

Seán and Sheila Ó Sé lived in the house three fields up the road and of their five children, Gerard and John were similar in age to Rupert and me so we quickly integrated. Three years after we arrived, the Carroll family – Frank, Marie and their young sons, Robert and Patrick – had decided on the big move to Kerry. They moved into a house behind Bealtra pier, a small fishing jetty that was awash at high tide and only four minutes down the road. The six of us lads were soon inseparable.

◄O►

One of Mum's first tasks was to teach us to swim and not to fear the water. A platform was made of wooden pallets lashed to a few empty oil drums and moored to the steep-sided rocky shore at the end of the garden. With a thick rope lashed around our waists, we all took our first plunge in the cold water of the harbour under the encouraging and watchful eyes of our parents. Soon after, a group of ladies from the Irish Countrywomen's Association toured the area and organised sea-swimming classes for all the local schoolchildren as part of an education programme to avert needless deaths in the fishing industry.

In deciding their parenting style, both our parents had deliberately opted not to do the one thing their own parents had done, notably, to discourage children from doing things they wanted to do – so they simply did the opposite, by extending trust and opportunity.

Dad's commute eventually paid a welcome dividend as the contacts he made along the route enabled him to start his own small practice working from home. Between this work and their small farm revenue, the modest income kept the books balanced as our parents realised their dream. The new location proved a wise choice thanks to the south-facing aspect, but the weather was easily as wild and rough. Living at the edge where land meets sea, one was always able to feel and hear the formidable rock face rumble in a very deep, distant, sonorous voice, mixed with the incessant cry of the seagulls. Although Derrynane enjoyed shelter from most wind directions, the narrow entrance between the rocks and small islands strewn across the mouth was tricky and became dangerous in the big ground seas that were the norm. The daily routine invariably started with curtains pulled back to check the sea state and whether our boats and our neighbours' had lasted the night.

—◄○►—

Mum was struggling to haul the punt around to push off the steep-sloping beach at Derrynane Pier. In spite of the warm sunshine, the freshening breeze was blowing across the harbour straight onto the beach, fighting her attempts to hold the bow into the wind and the steep chop. She could have opted to jump into the boat with stern to the sea but the small though mighty Seagull engine would have struggled against the wind and wavelets combined. Besides, the groceries stacked neatly on the floorboards would have been saturated.

I sat watching the proceedings patiently, enthroned athwart ships with Rupert. We had seen this played out many times before. Shortly, Mum would win the battle and we would be on our way home for a few chores before supper. Except that this battle didn't have to be fought alone.

'For goodness sake, Damian, get up off your bum and help me!' she cried. 'You're old enough and big enough now. Get the engine started.'

Although I was taken aback by Mum's tone, I jumped to the stern and quickly primed the engine as I had been shown and had practised with Dad before. Rupert looked on; his turn would come eventually but I was six now and it was my time.

The engine responded and we were soon on our way towards Bealtra and the mooring off the field at Bunavalla. The spray from the waves soon eased as we neared the far shore that was calmer in the shelter of the land, and the dried water left our faces encrusted with salt.

Later that evening, after bedtime but before the sun had set, the early summer gale arrived with full force. Lying awake in bed, I couldn't sleep as the afternoon's events replayed in my head. It had been a first, not just under strict supervision but actually a first when I was needed to take responsibility for an important part of managing our boat. New possibilities were definitely opening up. Perhaps I might now be allowed to take the boat on my own, maybe just row it and eventually use the engine. I decided to ask permission at the weekend, when Dad returned from Tralee or maybe when we were out fishing, if the gale had cleared by then. The horizons seemed boundless: Rupert, Ger, John, Robert and Patrick would join in for sure; whether motoring or rowing, we could cross the harbour and land like pirates on a distant island – the crescent-shaped cove on the eastern side would be ideal – where explorations would begin and treasure of all kinds would be hidden.

As the skies darkened and night fell, the distant sound of waves was dimmed by the sound of rain on the corrugated iron roof of my bedroom and brought sleep to my tired eyes. The summer ahead would be special, with new challenges and plenty of adventure.

3

The Derrynane Years

The gusting wind whipped up a short, choppy sea on top of a slow, heaving swell. A gale was brewing and would be with us by nightfall so the pressure was on to haul our pots or risk losing them and the catch. If we delayed, whatever pocket money Gerard and I could have brought in would surely have been lost as well as the valuable fishing gear.

Ger's father, Sean Ó Sé, had lent us the smaller of his two boats, an 18-foot wooden open punt, so we could fish for crayfish and lobsters. We had set our line of pots close to Hogs Head at the entrance to Ballinskelligs Bay, at the limit of our range from Derrynane and about as remote and wild as the Kerry coastline could offer, thanks to the formidable cliff faces broken only by a series of caves and rocky inlets.

But the backwash of the seas was getting rougher and even for two supposedly fearless thirteen-year-olds, we knew we lacked Sean Ó's years of experience and had to

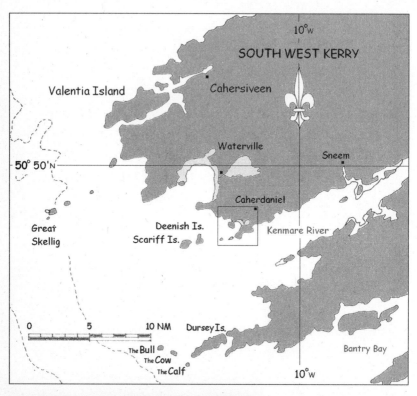

SOUTH WEST KERRY

10°w

Valentia Island

Cahersiveen

Waterville

Sneem

50° 50'N

Caherdaniel

Great
Skellig

Deenish Is.
Scariff Is.

Kenmare River

0   5   10 NM   Dursey Is.

Bantry Bay

The **Bull**
The **Cow**
The **Calf**

10°w

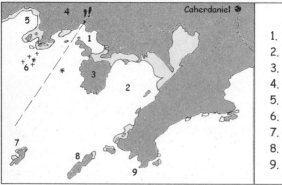

Caherdaniel

1. Derrynane Harbour
2. Derrynane Bay
3. Abbey Island
4. Bunavalla
5. Cuas na Gamhar
6. The Pigs
7. Moylaun Island
8. Two Headed Island
9. Lamb's Head

work quickly to get home. At least the 4-mile passage would be easier under the shelter of the cliffs.

With half the pots on board and stacked along the bench, progress was good until we found an unwelcome stowaway in the third from last pot. A conger eel, black and slimy, scowling its displeasure at finding itself on board, was slithering around the trap. We were none too happy either, though the challenge was clear. Had Sean Ó himself been on board, it would have been a cinch – just stick your hand in, grab it by the back of the head and flick it overboard. But this fella was at least as big as anything we'd seen before – hardly an anaconda but still about a metre long – and neither Ger nor I seemed able to dodge its fast-moving head and sharp fangs. The solution seemed to be to tip the pot overboard and let the conger slip away. But the swell made movement on the small boat clumsy and, instead of going overboard, the eel was now slithering around the bilge beneath the slatted deck planks and would pop its head up in different places, taunting and poised as if to attack before suddenly vanishing again. We pressed ahead with getting the remaining pots on board but the passenger was posing more of a threat and required disposal.

'C'mon, get the fecker, Damian!' roared Ger with a delighted grin as he hauled on the line of pots.

'You get him with the oar,' I retorted, forgetting that the oars were buried beneath all the pots and gear.

Having failed to grab the eel, I next tried stamping on its head to stun it when it appeared on the floorboards, but missed. As the boat lurched on a wave and the bilge water sloshed around the inside of the boat, I stomped hard but missed the conger again. Except this time, I put my foot through the wooden plank and holed the boat just below the waterline. I recalled Sean Ó's stern words advising us to always stand on the wood stringers and not the hull planks, which would not bear sudden heavy weight.

Seawater gushed through the foot-wide hole in the boat and, with every heave in the swell, threatened to swamp us completely. We stuffed our oilskin coats into the gap and tried to keep that side of the boat from ducking under water too much by shifting the weight of pots to the opposite side but to little avail. And all the while, the conger would pop its head or tail up as it roamed around wondering when it too would be free of us.

'Ah Jeesus, we're fecked now, Dad'll kill us!' shouted Ger, though I knew full well he meant I'd cop the blame, thanks to my boot. Somewhere on board, our life jackets floated around – despite our assurances to our parents that we'd always wear them – and the situation looked increasingly desperate; we had to get to shore and fast.

I struggled to drag the oars out from beneath the weight of gear while Gerard tried to get the small outboard engine going. It eventually obliged and spluttered into life. The knee-deep water in the boat meant there was no way we would last as far as Derrynane with any amount of bailing or even luck. A gap in the steep line of cliffs by Hogs Head revealed a flattish rock, relatively smooth and rising steadily from the water's edge above the high-water mark and the makings of a pathway above it to the higher ground seemed a possible solution.

We turned and gunned the engine hard and, with last-minute timing, owing more to luck than skill, we managed to surf our sinking boat on the surge of the swell, hitting the rock and riding the slippy lower reaches upwards until our momentum ran out and a sickening, grinding noise told us that we now had a second hole in the hull. Tumbling out of the boat, we rested atop the large rock to catch our breath. We were at least safe and had got the boat and gear ashore. That was the good news but we had still to tell Sean Ó and face a 10-mile trek home to Bunavalla.

After struggling off the rock, we called to a nearby farmhouse. The elderly couple there had seen our landing so helped out with a hot drink and use of their phone to call our parents. As we set out for home, the negotiations began as we started to fix our story to explain how, without lying, an important part of Sean Ó's livelihood was nearly completely written off. There would be no escaping a thorough bollocking once we returned and to be honest we were shitting ourselves, or more exactly, I was. Anything we could add to the story, short of actually admitting to causing the boat to be holed, would be vital to escape a more serious sanction. In the end, we opted to omit the detail of how the boat was holed and to embellish how we managed to avoid a total loss.

After the gale had passed, we went out with Sean Ó on his other boat in the company of a neighbour, Kevin Patsey, and his fishing boat to refloat the punt, which was repaired and returned to work. And so our story held and we even managed to have a laugh about it over the years with Seán Ó as, bit by bit, the whole truth emerged and became part of the patchwork of stories that was our childhood.

◄◦►

To be fair, fixing the story between myself and Ger was more banter than barter but if I owed him for covering my part in the holing Sean Ó's punt, it also was probably repayment for some other incident along the way. It wasn't that we were ever troublemakers or deliberately set out to create mischief, but kids being kids, nearly always someone was up for a prank. When we were younger, our primary school teacher, Maureen Moran, would drive us to and from school in Caherdaniel in her small minibus. Our meeting point was on the 'high road' under the crest of the mountain overlooking Bunavalla valley, which stretched in a green blanket of fields and farms all the way down to the harbour below. On our return journey, getting back from the main road involved a zigzagging road up the hill, passing each house where our group would grow smaller.

Any short cut we could take to lessen the walk was taken, including through the collection of whitewashed old stone buildings that was the farmyard belonging to Cait and Ger Galvin, an elderly farming couple whose hay barn was always well stocked and offered plenty of distractions for bored children homeward bound, with little interest in chores or studies. Cait and Ger were super neighbours and especially kind to our family with advice for our parents and their small farm. Homes were never locked and even in the worst weather the front doors were generally left open and visitors were always welcome. Cait would often have us in for a cup of tea along with her sister Mary and Ger's brother Jim who lived with them and they would all would call to us at Christmas.

Though the large barn was off-limits, six of us were playing inside making houses and towers of hay bales and being careful to keep noise to a minimum lest we give ourselves away. Our own Gerard, unbeknownst to the rest of us, had snuck outside, found a plank of wood and started banging it along the corrugated steel cladding on the outside of the barn. We froze at the din and instantly knew both that the game was up and who was responsible.

Cait appeared at the door of the farmhouse as we dived to hide amongst the bales. But it was no use: Ger continued his racket before darting away outside the farmyard to watch the unfolding drama. Fearing the worst – teenagers experimenting with cigarettes and matches – Cait yelled for help.

'They're in the barn,' she yelled. 'Quick, do something before the place goes up in flames!'

'I will, I will,' replied the elderly Ger who arrived at her side, pulling on his cap. 'I'll get Kevin Patsey to them, he'll sort them out.'

Their neighbour was as quiet and gentle a man as any but his giant size and huge hands terrified us as he strode in, with Cait and Ger taking up the rear. One by one, he discovered our hiding places and was soon busy grabbing neck scruffs and hauling us out of the barn.

'Go on away out off that,' he growled with a wink.

'You're not to be coming into our yard again,' screeched Cait as we tried to duck Kevin Patsey's hands and sprint towards the gate where young Ger was waiting innocently, blameless unlike the rest of us. We fled the farmyard and berated Ger as he hooted his delight at our expense and the tit-for-tat battle rolled on.

Such antics were only distractions as our real interests revolved around the shoreline and waters of Derrynane

Harbour that bordered the Caherdaniel townland near the southern slopes of Cahernageeha Mountain. My group of friends was gathered from the immediate area of Bunavalla that nestles beside the harbour at Bealtra and our natural playground also featured dozens of 4,000-year-old megalithic tombs and fairy forts, offering both mystery and a sense of place. Parental supervision was discreet but on very clear lines – cross the boundaries and privileges would be withdrawn. We were warned to be careful on the cliffs and, from a young age always to wear a life jacket when playing on boats.

A favourite if risky game was down by the sea, rolling large stones down 100-metre-long slab rock faces to bomb into the breaking waves below, or sprinting up and down the same lichen-covered faces that sloped away into the sea. We loved it when the winds whipped up great frothy fields of aerated water, soup-thick and yellowish brown in colour that defied the undertow and wouldn't dissipate. These waves of foam, up to 4 metres in height in the coves, were thrown up the shore where we would try and time a last-minute sprint from harm, too often being caught in the midst of the suffocating goo but eventually emerging like off-colour snowmen.

Games would range across the entire valley and beyond the woods into the next valley, Derrynane woodlands, sand dunes and the National Park – the estate home of Daniel O'Connell, the Liberator – and into our village, Caherdaniel itself. We had Chopper bikes, complete with back-pedal brakes and high saddles but, though they were vital for independence, the steep-sided hill meant we could not go far quickly and were almost always faster on foot.

It was a tightly knit group of friends, despite the age difference that spanned three or four years. Occasional scraps were usually in jest but we avoided anything more serious, probably due to the huge space our natural playground offered to express ourselves in. We were free and we had the valley to ourselves.

Winter was more restricting and with no television until we were much older, we were denied such delights as *Chitty Chitty Bang Bang* at Christmas or *Dallas,* which seemed to be the talk of the schoolyard from the homes that had access to rural Ireland's then limited two-channel national broadcasts. Later on, we were allowed half an hour's viewing daily but the box held little attraction by then. It wasn't that TV was a bad thing, we just had too much else to do.

We lived for summertime and the fun it brought, sun-baked days with long evenings and warm nights that always came too soon. Irish holidays are simply the best in the world – *three* whole months off school, traditionally intended to allow children to help out on the farm. We rose early and keenly to get our chores finished before lunchtime, and to have the rest of the day to ourselves. The haymaking season was the exception when the days were spent turning the hay before the chance of summer rain, and we would work late into the evenings until it was done.

At weekends, we looked forward to the expeditions Dad and Mum would arrange. Mountainous ridges, hidden bays with off-lying islands and deep woodlands are what make southwest Kerry and we had an endless supply of new territory to explore on our day trips, sometimes camping overnight. Our parents were natural outdoor types and their love of nature passed easily on to us. And although we tried, we never physically managed to travel as far as our boundless imaginations wanted to take us.

For some reason, Mum wasn't with us on a Saturday walking trip in the deep woods between Sneem and Kenmare when we arrived at a cliff inlet near Blackwater where a massive pine tree had fallen across the gap and seemed to shout 'Bridge Here' to the path-finding party of Rob, Patrick, Rupert and me. The tree's trunk was certainly wide enough to cross but torn roots and rotten branches presented a clear risk. One trip and a fall into the gully and surging surf below would certainly have been fatal.

A glance back to Dad was returned with a look that simply said 'Go on then. Just be careful . . .'

It spoke volumes about how our parents viewed us and their determination that we should take responsibility for our own decisions – and the consequences of those decisions. Offloading the blame to others was not an option. A lot of parents certainly would not have allowed it but Dad reckoned if a child wants to do something then better help him do it well, discover where the limits are in advance so eventually the child develops his own skill set. Hopefully, there would not be too many injuries or slip-ups along the way. In the same way, they were not strict disciplinarians and punishments were balanced – it was unusual to be smacked, even by the standards of the day.

We had been allowed to row the family punt around Derrynane Harbour from around the age of ten, under the clear understanding we would wear life jackets. After Mum's early lessons, we were strong enough swimmers to reach the punt without needing to bring it ashore on its outhaul tackle. Shortly after arriving in Derrynane, my father had bought a 12-foot Gunter-rigged dinghy to teach Rupert and me to sail. It was hand-built of steam-moulded marine ply by the Rankin brothers in Cobh, County Cork, one of whom was blind but masterfully created his work boats by touch.

Along with the punt, the Rankin gave us free access to the harbour and later the full coastline. Eventually permission was granted to use the Seagull engine and great seaborne expeditions from Derrynane Harbour commenced. The test for this was demonstrating that we were strong enough oarsmen to row off a lee shore should the engine fail. Even in the midst of the frequent near gale force winds we were relatively well sheltered usually and, with caution, could navigate the choppy waves. But a lee shore outside the confines of the harbour was very dangerous, even in fresh winds, which were typical in the summer months. And in the southwest gales, the entrance was completely exposed. All the time, we were constantly urged to consider the weather and the possibilities of things going against us and how we might adapt to the new situation.

It was a location that offered huge possibilities, whether for fun, adventure or even business opportunities. A fairly regular occurrence would be a visiting yacht misjudging the entrance to the harbour and ending up banging against the rocks. That was when the punt came in handy and the view from the house overlooking the bay provided an early-warning lookout post.

In those days I hadn't realised that, to have a claim of salvage over a stricken vessel, the imperilled crew needed to take your tow line for a valid claim. Nevertheless, the occasional rescue operation would invariably result in a coke at Bridie's Bar and perhaps a quid or two as a gesture of thanks and I doubt salvage would have entered our minds even had we known about it.

But other commercial ventures held hope of steadier funds. Despite odd looks from older fishermen at our obedient life-jacket routine, Robert and I managed to fish lobsters and periwinkles that sold for £15 a bag. Fresh fruit and vegetables from the garden could also be negotiated with the visiting yachts. Our ambitions knew no end and at one stage we attended a seminar on the fledgling industry of aquaculture that soon had us hanging lines from small buoys moored outside the harbour in an attempt to encourage mussels to grow. Within years, it took off on the Kenmare river in a big way but without any involvement for our fledgling Carroll, Foxall and Co. fish company. In winter months, we generated pocket money by picking periwinkles and clearing rhododendron that was strangling the natural woodland around Lord Dunraven's estate in Derrynane. We were not allowed to use chainsaws so with Bushman saws and axes progress was painfully slow and our money was well earned.

It was at that stage, when unsupervised forays outside the protection of Derrynane Harbour started increasing, that new parental strictures governing the basics of passage planning were applied. Back-up plans were always needed to cater for the unexpected and several drownings in the area served as sobering reminders from time to time. Otherwise, it was safe enough, provided the precautions were in place.

Summertime brought more and more visitors holidaying to the area and the Splash Bash in Derrynane Harbour of today started as a great treasure hunt and maritime festival in the 1980s that we all joined in. From my early savings, I bought a windsurfer and, along with the lads, spent any free time on the water, whatever the season and right through the winter. Ossie and Helen Wilson started a sailing school and we were determined to become instructors. Helen had moved to Derrynane when she was fourteen, met Ossie at the local youth club when she was seventeen and they were married at twenty-two. He was a sailor who had started out on Laser and Fireball dinghies until one day he was passed out by a windsurfer and he switched to the exciting sport of boardsailing. Both had the same dynamic zest for life and pleasure as they had for working with people and they started out their school with seven boards and a Hiace van, eventually expanding to canoes, Lasers and a waterski boat. Along with the normal fishing activities and the odd visiting yachts the harbour now came alive.

Dad was now working from home and the family fleet increased substantially with the arrival of *Canna*, a first series, glass-fibre production Nicholson 32-footer. Funded by a legacy from Mum's late father it was fitting that passing his own passion for the ocean to his family was to be continued even after his death. *Canna* would now open up an extended world of cruising opportunities and we all were involved. Dad tried to charter *Canna* out to visitors but the weather could rarely be properly relied upon and was deceptive more often than cooperative so he usually ended up skippering it himself for them.

On one family day trip, Dad spotted that unusually calm weather had left the beach at Cuas na Gamhar completely clear of breakers and we had an opportunity to explore an area that was normally inaccessible. Massive boulders had piled together to form caves and cracks lined the back of a narrow tidal beach. Steep-sided cliffs barricaded both ends of the beach, which was the only access point. Anchoring the punt just off the shore, we were able to swim ashore on bodyboards and explore the caves that lined the bottom of the cliffs. We had barely arrived when a crashing wave announced the arrival of a train of swells, which threatened to wreck the boat and maroon us beyond help ahead of the incoming tide.

I had swum out to the boat and had been riding out the first swell sitting on the bow so I was just able to lift the anchor and get the engine started to pick up the others from the water as the surf returned, heralding a distant storm possibly coming our way. With the boat swamped but floating – just – we hurriedly abandoned the Cuas and returned to more forgiving waters at Derrynane before the conditions completely revolted against us.

Outside the protection of Derrynane Harbour, three small islands nestled offshore, within an easy day's sail provided the weather cooperated. The smaller island, called Moylaun, was slightly separated from Scariff and neighbouring Deenish Island, which was uninhabited except for a small house with the door left on the latch by its absentee owner who generously permitted day trippers to shelter there provided they signed the visitors' book and left the place tidy and rubbish free. The high rocky island, with a natural cove and soft grass leading up to the ruins, was an ideal destination for family expeditions and an annual summer event as friends and neighbours met over a fire on the beach to barbeque freshly caught mackerel, all within sight of the boats lying to anchor in the small cove.

◄○►

On a trip to Deenish Island, Rob and I had brought coils of old mooring rope with us and made up some rusty steel pegs to enable a proper exploration of the island's cliffs on the south face. With base camp established by our parents, we were free to begin our operations well out of sight. Shortly after the last peg had been driven into the ground and we had dropped the rope over the cliff, Dad arrived, presumably having noticed our absence for an hour or two.

'How are you getting on?' he enquired politely, ignoring the fact that the rope and gear had apparently been smuggled onto the island.

'Grand, thanks,' we replied, and explained the planned survey.

Inspired by Chris Bonnington's climbing accomplishments on Annapurna and Everest, we had a plan or so we thought. Dad listened patiently and with interest, sidestepping the facts that abseiling was an acquired skill or that we had not set up a safety line.

'You've got the length of rope, all right,' he murmured, peering carefully over the grass edge and down the slab and the 90-foot drop towards the crashing waves in the kelp below. 'And it'll be interesting to see if there are any nests along the crevices. Well, I'm off for lunch, enjoy yourselves,' he added as he turned to head for the beach. 'Hope you've got good grip on your boots; that weed at the bottom won't be easy to climb back up.'

We were left in silence as he continued his walk. Our plan hadn't been so complete after all and we were now faced with a dilemma – make the descent and risk injury or stranding if the climb failed, or abandon the project and find another, more reliable activity for the afternoon. In the end, we made the sensible choice and found another cliff face that gave us a safer escape option. I imagine that my father must have walked away praying fervently that his discreet message had found its target.

The island had changed hands through the local community many times over the years and an Englishman was its most recent purchaser. On arrival, he found that the Indian summer had left the well quite dry so he stretched out a large sheet of tarpaulin on the grass between the rocks to catch whatever rainwater he could. When we arrived onto the island one morning, we were part of a bigger company of people that included Alex, another Englishman who was a semi-permanent resident during the summer months. He was a gregarious man with a booming voice as big as his Land Rover and an old overfed black Labrador. As everyone settled down to a picnic, the Lab waddled off to find a convenient spot to relieve itself but instead came across the tarpaulin, which had been filling nicely and was almost full. The dog decided that was his spot to relieve himself. The normally absentee landlord just happened to be present that weekend and was horrified at the ruined water supply and a noisy row ensued between the two Englishmen that ended with Alex heading back to his boat and the mainland.

◄○►

Our parents' theories of allowing children space for initiative and common sense to develop required a measure of trial and error with little chance of assured outcomes. While they were outwardly permissive, sanctions had to be held in reserve and applied as needed, ultimately to serve as some form of deterrent centred on loss of privileges such as being barred from going out on the dinghy or windsurfer. Because of this, it was rare enough to have difficulties.

Still, the freedom of summer never lasted long enough and when I entered my teenage years, it was clear that my relationship with school was problematic. The issue was, simply, that it got in the way of being outside doing more interesting things and because of that, I didn't like it much. Later on, when it became obvious that a career as a professional windsurfer was apparently destiny calling, the frustration only intensified. For Pat, repairing motorbikes clearly showed his technical capabilities. As I watched Ossie shaping his own boards, 'guns' that we tested in the squally conditions of Derrynane Harbour, I knew that even sailing in the depths of winter appealed to me. And if the best thing was being on the water taking part, the next best was helping others to get going, so teaching was a natural calling.

But being 'schooled' was a different situation. It had not been apparent or mattered so much in primary school. We liked our teacher Mrs Moran and enjoyed the sports we played there, such as handball on Saturdays or running races in the back field where we also played Gaelic football. This was especially important as Ger and John's father, Sean Ó, was dedicated to county football, had played alongside the great Mick O'Dwyer and when he wasn't bringing us to cross-country running meets, he would take us to training sessions and to see the Kerry greats in action.

Everyone in the area knew Micko – there was no need to ask for a last name thanks to his fourteen-year career as a county player followed by fifteen years as arguably the most successful manager of all time. As we grew up we came to know him instantly, then later recognised the career he made from sport that also, somehow, included a business and family. Aside from football, Sean Ó and Micko were great friends and fished together even during peak championship season. For the past two decades, Micko's boat has been the *St Malachy*, a 20-foot open punt maintained by his Uncle Batt, but many years before he had taken to the sea itself to prove a myth true. Scariff was a large formidable high island with green sloping sides, good for grazing but even without a single stretch of flat land it was still habitable. Originally owned by descendants of Daniel O'Connell before passing to the Butlers of Waterville, our neighbour Batt Galvin was born there. During the birth of his sister there were complications and medical help was needed urgently. Batt's father swam the 3 miles to the mainland to get help. The baby girl grew up to become Micko's mother.

However, the story of the open-water swim took on mythical overtones, such was the feat of endurance involved. After some provocation by Sean Ó, Micko had had enough. With his pal following discreetly with his boat in case cramps took hold, Micko swam the distance and quickly proved that it could, in fact, be done and let there be no further doubt about that.

But the incident highlighted the problems with living on an offshore island and not long afterwards the Galvins moved off the island. The Ó Sé family took over occupancy until 1932 when they too came ashore and bought land on the mainland. Batt-Larry Ó Sé owned a smallholding with five acres in Bunavalla and it was this house and land that my parents bought in the early 1970s.

◄○►

After the freedom of primary school, secondary school came as a shock. As the eldest by one year of all the friends, I was first to leave the valley and head in the opposite direction. The options were limited. Girls went to the nuns in Cahersiveen while boys could attend the Christian Brothers there or go to the 'Tech' in Waterville, which is where I ended up. Rob and Pat went to the Brothers the following year while Ger and Rupert joined me at the Tech.

But for that first year alone, waiting for the school bus at the top of the hill, the only other child was a girl who terrified me so much we never spoke to each other once in the entire year. Waterville Tech was pleasant enough but each start of autumn term, as the sun blazed through the classroom windows, the blue skies proved hugely distracting after a summer of windsurfing, sailing and the great outdoors.

Mechanical Drawing and Woodwork proved exceptions to the humdrum of academia and the two subjects received my best attention, resulting usually in A and B grades. Only those serious about the subject were tolerated in the Woodwork class; others opted to take Home Economics, some because it offered easy grades while others had other motives amongst the girls.

Our Woodwork teacher was Mr O'Sullivan who was close to retirement and whose son also taught at the school. He was a large man with a gentle manner and a passion for his work, which included maintaining a wooden boat and a beautifully equipped workshop for his classes. He commanded great respect from his students that rarely slipped. On the one occasion it did, the dubious honour fell to Paudie Murphy who was a little older and much bigger than the rest of the class. He was the nearest we had to a 'hard man' in the school, dressed in a mod-parka, and had a 'don't start with me' air. Nobody bothered to test him and we all got along fine.

Murphy had been fiddling around with some equipment at the back of the class and O'Sullivan noticed immediately. Pausing mid-speech, he calmly picked up a large wooden mallet from our bench, lifted it level with his eye, as if to take aim. My pal Michael Curran and I, seated in the front-row bench, sensed what was coming and leaned apart as the weighty hammer was launched between us towards the back wall where it landed safely. Murphy's face turned white as O'Sullivan traversed the classroom of kids and woodwork benches in the blink of an eye and lifted him by the scruff of his shirt and held him back against the wall. In

Roger Foxall. (Foxall family)

Susan Foxall *née* Stanley. (Foxall family)

Damian's grandfather Frank Stanley. (Foxall family)

Traditional Star class clinker boats on a fresh afternoon. (Foxall family)

Picnic on Deenish Island, *c.* 1980, with (l–r) Susan, Rupert and Damian.
(Foxall family)

Canna, a Nicholson 32. (Foxall family)

Damian and his mother, Susan, in Montserrat in 1993. (Foxall family)

Damian during the single-handed Solitaire du Figaro.
(Courtesy Thierry Martinez/Sea & Co)

Celebrating
first place in the
Solitaire du Figaro
leg arriving into
Concarneau.

(Courtesy
Benoît Stichelbaut)

Deep in the Southern Ocean on board *Team Tyco* during the
2001–2002 Volvo Ocean Race. (Foxall family)

Racing with Ellen MacArthur on *Kingfisher B&Q* in 2003.
(*Courtesy* Jacques Vapillon)

Heading for the finish line at Ushant with Steve Fossett on *Cheyenne*.
(*Courtesy* Thierry Martinez/Sea&Co)

Start of the Transat Jacques Vabre on *Foncia* with Armel le Cléac'h.
(*Courtesy* Thierry Martinez/Sea&Co)

Celebrating third place in the Transat Jacques Vabre with Karine Fauconnier.
(*Courtesy* Benoît Stichelbaut)

ORMA 60-footer *Sergio Tacchini* in 2003.
(*Courtesy* Benoît Stichelbaut)

the heat of the moment, it seemed to us that Murphy had levitated clear off the ground aided only by a light grip and O'Sullivan's stern look.

'Never, ever mess in my class again,' he said and continued with a pointed diatribe delivered in low tones on the hazards of the heavy tools around the workshop and the harm they might cause to the unwary. There was no margin for mistakes and we all understood. Murphy didn't mess again; nor did anyone else, for that matter. The classes were too good to miss or mess in and we were ten times better off for our teacher's interest and care for his subject. We learnt more about respect and limits from him than any other teacher; and that was without him ever directly raising the subject.

◄○►

Teenage life in south Kerry rolled on, as ever hinged around the beach and the sea, getting into boats and staying out of trouble, living for the summer, which was flanked by a sense of anticipation in the spring months and later a buzzing momentum that carried long into winter.

Waterville Tech became the centre of activities during the weekdays in term-time and a small group of classmates hung out together, enduring the boring subjects and revelling in the hands-on classes as well as sports after hours. The minute classes ended, we played Gaelic handball – real handball, unlike European handball, which is more like basketball for continental dudes who can't jump. But, given a choice, we would still prefer to head for the playing fields to practise football. Twenty of us would line up at either end of the pitch and kick balls to one another; whoever fielded the ball would kick it back to the other end, blasting the ball constantly between the two groups. When it came to Gaelic football, no other county in Ireland could match 'the Kingdom': Kerry had won the Sam Maguire Cup more than twenty times, far more than any other team in the Senior Football Championship. Four consecutive wins in the early 1980s only served to copper-fasten the self-belief that unified our mini-nation, which had been a stronghold of the sport since the earliest days of Caid, a forerunner of Gaelic football, in the fourteenth century.

Scarcely a corner of the county went untouched by supporter mania in some form or another, especially when it came to matches. For us, science class held a special incentive as the Eoin 'the Bomber' Liston was our teacher, a man of legendary status with a 6 foot 3 inch frame who played for the county team at the peak of its winning run and was noted as one of the greatest forwards in the history of the modern game.

Both Mick O'Dwyer and the Bomber Liston typified the amateur spirit of the game: fitter than many pros in other sports *and* able carry on a full-time job. A wage packet was not their motivation and the followers loved them all the more for it. When Kerry won the championship, we were all champions and the excitement spread to every person there.

Whether on the pitch or off, as a player or follower, Kerry united behind its players' achievements and generated a massive momentum of support. It was and is everything you could ask for – roots and sport together, everyone involved and so connected that the county would come to a virtual halt on match day. Without a television in the house, we would gather around a radio or head to a neighbour's to watch the game and if ever it might have come to a choice between windsurfing or football as a career, in pure sporting terms my heart lay with the county. Although I was useful enough on the football field and was selected for some inter-parish games as well, I lacked the natural aptitude that the best players had for running at full tilt down the field, chipping the ball off the ground before soloing down the pitch and delivering it straight through the posts and all without losing speed; a beautiful thing.

There was good inter-parish rivalry and because of their small populations, the Derrynane team included Castlecove. Neighbouring Sneem always fielded a team along with Waterville and Cahersiveen and our victories were always cherished. Living in the area made participation in sport almost a certainty. Of our group at home, it was Ger and I who usually joined Sean Ó to go to the senior matches along with his younger children, Mark, Louise and Elaine; the Ó Sé family were a true sport-mad family.

—◄○►—

Batt Galvin was one of a handful of older men – Small Johnny, Big Johnny, Jim Galvin, Dan Sean Sheamus and Jim Jackeen – who were all committed bachelors but held in quiet respect by everyone in the area: great men who typified the simplicity of traditional life on the west coast of Ireland. This was the same background that Tom Crean had come from, and we grew up reading the Shackleton polar expedition stories. 'Men wanted for hazardous journey. Small wages, bitter cold, long months of complete darkness, constant journey, safe return doubtful. Honour and recognition in case of success.' So read the advertisement placed by Ernest Shackleton in a London newspaper in August 1914. It is said that 5,000 people responded to it.

Batt lived in a small cottage which was well kept but for a rotting front door. Lanky and with a gaunt appearance that hinted at a younger life as a tall athletic man, he had a permanent heavy limp and a hawthorn stick that he used both for walking and as an effective device for putting extra passion and emphasis into his prose. From his porch, he had the best views around and could look down the valley over the fields to Derrynane Harbour.

After receiving his fortnightly dole payment, he would go walkabout for a few days in the area, calling on friends and neighbours to catch up on news and gossip. His favourite bar stool in the pub was kept free for his imminent arrival for a late night pint or two and if an unsuspecting visitor happened to take the place, that person would be politely though firmly invited to select another spot. As soon as we were able to go roaming around by ourselves, Batt's cottage was a regular stop. He was a font of knowledge and had great tales that ranged from football to fishing. A lot of what we thought we knew or imagined about girls was passed on from him as part of various innocent stories he delighted in telling us.

Batt kept two large kettles in his kitchen: one full of water, the other of diesel. If ever we arrived and the fire wasn't lit, we would build up the sods of turf as he brought out the two kettles to the fireplace. First the diesel would be emptied over the turf. 'Stand back, lads,' he would call before throwing a lit match onto some newspapers to ignite a roaring fire. The kettle of water was hung over the fire and while we waited for the tea to brew, Batt would reappear with a loaf of soda bread tucked under his arm. He took out a butter knife so sharp that in a single swipe he could slice a piece of bread to be served up with a slab of butter almost as thick as the bread itself as we settled in to discuss our important business.

As we got older but before drinking age, the cups of tea turned to whiskey, and Batt, who never seemed to age, kept us entertained with his great turns of phrase. This evening, the conversation somehow drifted onto the subject of condoms. Typically undeterred, whatever the conversation, Batt offered his unique observation:

'In my day, we had no condoms, only a glass of whiskey by the bed,' he remarked, leaving us to ponder the magical properties of the *uisce beatha*.

Though our parents were not from the Gaelic tradition, our mother especially encouraged us to be caught up in the awesome tide of support for the county team. It was the cross-country running that became our regular activity with Mum, who took us training to the field behind the house, setting up a sprint track to time our laps and coach our style. While games were all very well for day-to-day distraction, occasionally matters might get a little out of hand, though never seriously and never harmfully. As the group got older, one-upmanship started to take hold and we were soon pushing one another to new levels.

Soon after our fifth year of secondary school started, we were enjoying the end of an Indian summer and happy to spend our lunch breaks outdoors. Farmers had been burning off furze in the mountains near the school and we were impressed by the fires each day. A new idea took hold and soon things started to get out of control. Our school was surrounded by bushes and other small trees and shrubs, so, one day, someone put a match to a small bush, which took light and burned steadily, leaving a pall of smoke hanging around the yard. The following day, another bush took fire, this time slightly bigger and a bug was catching on.

Towards the end of the week, Travers and I used a cigarette lighter on a clump of dead leaves at the base of a hedge of flaggers to see if we could generate some more decent smoke but were disappointed to find it simply smouldered and didn't burn. Shrugging it off, we returned for afternoon lessons, into the hot classroom where direct sunlight blazed in and almost guaranteed lethargy.

Soon after class started, we heard the deep rumble that sounded like the rain on the prefab roof. However, this was out of place on a summer day and we heard the racket of people shouting and running through the schoolyard. In the distance, the fire brigade was racing to the scene. Looking out, we could see water hoses being run out and over the roof of the other school building. Flames were leaping up from the evergreen hedge that surrounded the school boundary and smoke filled the air. It seemed that the resin-filled hedge and our bunch of dead leaves had been significantly more flammable than we could ever have imagined. And as we now stood in the courtyard looking at the mayhem it felt like life was about to change. The school was evacuated until the fire was brought under control and the entire hedge was reduced to a cinder.

The following day, an investigation got under way. Every single student was interviewed, some twice and stories were cross-checked to get to the bottom of the incident and identify the fire starters. Travers and I blatantly denied any knowledge of the cause, though the names of the culprits had spread quicker than the fire itself. Eventually, two first-year kids let it slip and we were hauled before the Principal Donnelly who promptly suspended us.

We had put him in a difficult position and he was really more than lenient. Despite our continued denials – after all, we had only lit some leaves, not wilfully torched the hedge – expulsion might have been more appropriate, but the more severe punishment was what we received at home, including being grounded. Of course, we had never intended setting the school on fire – it never even crossed our minds. We just wanted some leaves to make smoke. But in our stupidity, we had failed to think the risks through fully or even appreciate that if things went wrong, we would be held accountable. Personal responsibility was just some classroom theory, right?

Wrong. In reality, we were close to being out of control and the whole episode served as a watershed, a peak of misbehaviour that was getting close to being a criminal offence and so required remedial action.

Principal Donnelly met with my parents in an attempt at stage an intervention to avoid a more serious outcome from further incidents.

'Damian isn't one of the Indians here,' he told them. 'But he is one of the chiefs.' It was time to switch me to a new environment before bad habits took hold and worse took place, he recommended. The solution was banishment and, as I had done wrong, I wasn't in a position to argue. After a serious conversation with my parents, who faced a considerable outlay for the fees, I was despatched to Bandon Grammar, a boarding school in west Cork originally founded in the seventeenth century – and almost three hours by road from Caherdaniel.

The basic goal was to get to college on the back of As and Bs from two years at Bandon, which I was more than capable of achieving but application was needed. The notion of studying marine biology in Galway appealed and since I could name almost any plant, animal and rock and many in Latin as well, and with my previous passing interest in aquaculture with Robert, there were grounds for optimism.

Although it was halfway through the first term, I set off on the journey with my father who spent much of the journey recalling bygone times, when a child younger than I would have left home to go to sea as a cadet in a tall ship, like a story from Patrick O'Brian's *Master and Commander* books set during the Napoleonic wars. Those were the good old days, when such things were possible without a formal education and when enthusiasm and aptitude would suffice to let fate take its course for a young man. But I remained a teenager from a small village in Kerry and the easy dream of becoming a professional windsurfer lived on as a stronger impulse than a vague commitment to a formal, academic path.

At Bandon Grammar, I was again stuck inside in a classroom learning irrelevant stuff (as I viewed it) that had little to do with my real career. The new school was an adventure and had new sports: hockey, which didn't appeal, and rugby, which was enjoyable though unfamiliar, but an injury stopped me taking it up seriously.

The change of scene did little to stop the rebellious side coming out, and with new friends I was often mitching class and leaving empty packets of 10 Major around the back of bike sheds. But the confines of boarding-school life and the hunger for the outdoors and adventure were too much. My dream had to be realised and I parted company with my formal education. Within a few months of leaving, I was home once again. Instead of giving me a grilling, my parents concluded that their best efforts had been made and it was time to let nature run its course.

It was late winter 1986, almost spring, which meant one thing: summer was coming. The beach and waters off Derrynane were already calling, skies would soon clear and the rough seas would ease. The wind would never stop, of course, but that excepted, change was in the air.

4

London Calling

Tralee Bus Station, 1986

If I was nervous, I didn't notice and was content to chat away to Mum as she drove me around the Ring of Kerry and up to Tralee to catch the bus. There was no emotional farewell or ceremony with Dad and Rupert, just another day in Derrynane except that I was off to London after another long and happy summer of sailing and wind-surfing. As friends continued at school, my bluff – if that's what it was – was being well and truly called. Yet, it was not a decision made lightly and there were plenty of discussions in the lead-up to the departure. Eventually, it boiled down to a simple choice presented by my parents: if you want to leave school now, off you go.

As we waited for the bus to depart, I sat by the window to look out at Mum waiting by the car park and still had no second thoughts. And an odd sense of something unusual was dismissed as just being part of the excitement of the start of the journey. After all, it was just another Irish seventeen-year-old following the well-worn path off the island to the neighbouring country in search of whatever he could find. There was no great master plan, no research or contact or even trace of work lined up at the other end. In short, I was clueless except for vague ideas gleaned from various books on working abroad: French vineyards, perhaps, or maybe apple-picking in Israel.

Certainly, there was little chance of windsurfing in either of these and even less of a chance on the streets of London where I was headed. This was what every kid did when they upped and took off into the big wide world and my plan – or rather lack of – was good enough to start off with. And London was the only realistic option anyway. The alternative might have been a flight from Shannon to America but that would have been hugely expensive and involved the complication of a green card.

The previous day I had visited the small post office in Waterville and cleared out one and a half savings book stamps. Together with some cash from my piggy bank, I had managed to bring a float of £150, which was safely stuffed into my pocket. As a family, we had operated a basic pocket-money system for essentials only so any savings were what was left over from teaching windsurfing or any part-time jobs we had. The trip to London was the first major expenditure since buying our windsurfer three years previously and the fund was precious.

As the CIÉ bus pulled away, I waved goodbye to my Mum who smiled sweetly and gave me a gentle wave, not once moving until the bus had altogether departed. I settled into my seat and prepared for the marathon, pain-in-the-ass journey ahead. From Tralee to Macroom it was stop-start, bouncing along the winding roads of Kerry and Cork and on to Waterford before taking the Rosslare-to-Pembroke ferry and the bus again to London with occasional stops at filling stations for driver breaks and food.

Any dipping into the funds was a hugely self-conscious act – London would not be cheap but it became a reminder that while I was not fully in control of my situation, it was part of something that I had initiated: what was happening was a direct result of my actions. For this fact alone, I was happy.

And as the journey wore on, the odd feeling inside returned and my mind cast back to the bus station in Tralee. It occurred to me that despite her typical calm, stoic appearance my mum might have actually been very upset. The moment had arrived, after years of her very best efforts, that her son was leaving to find his own path. I had their blessings and support, and knew it would work out, in time. But with a sudden impact, the enormity of the step I was taking finally dawned.

London

The initial days in London were a mix of culture shock and exploration. First priority was accommodation and after drifting towards Earl's Court as so many of the travel books had advised, I wandered around and found shops and phone boxes filled with advertising leaflets, mostly for hookers and a few for rooms to let and hostels.

It was in the days before backpacking became popular and the hostel was a dump. It was clear that while dirt in the country is clean dirt, city dirt is just plain filthy. The first night was especially unpleasant and I awoke from a nightmare in a cold sweat to be told to shut up by an irritated Aussie.

By day, I wandered the streets of London for hours, criss-crossing roads, looking at buildings and sights, getting lost and un-lost, all the time finding my way around. I hardly gained cabbies' 'knowledge' although even without a map I soon became orientated and comfortable. And all the time, fully aware of my funds dwindling at the (relatively) expensive hostel.

Eventually, I found a cheap bedsit in Kilburn and moved in within a few days of arriving in London. Amongst the other tenants were two lads from Waterford who worked on building sites and shared the room next to mine while downstairs were two girls. We did not see all that much of each other but one of the lads was very put out when his mate received an invitation to join the girls for an evening of 'fun and entertainment'. He was left to his own devices or stay in and listen to the goings-on in the room below.

My traipsing around the streets and London Underground eventually brought me to Piccadilly Circus, which turned out to be an epicentre of the more colourful side of London life. Rent boys for example, were an eye-opener and something new altogether – not a feature you might come across in Caherdaniel. Still, I landed a job paying £1.75 an hour at a Wimpy burger joint, which, given its location, was supposedly the biggest and busiest in Britain with a huge turnover. New recruits started by sweeping and cleaning and we eventually learnt to make burgers. Although the pay was basic, it was money that would pay rent and a little extra, maybe. Better still, you got to eat twice per shift so by working hard and well it became a way to economise. Plus, I could just afford to take driving lessons.

Whether it was Wimpy or London or a combination of both, the staff was a great mix of nationalities and cultures. There were lots of Africans and West Indians and as I made a lot of friends, especially in the black community, there were plenty of house parties in Clapham and Brixton to attend. Although I had been to London once before with my mother, these were the first coloured people I had ever encountered and I was soon able to confirm that they were otherwise identical to everyone else of whatever skin hue. Many people working there were students as well though some opted to move on and become supervisors. This was something I considered but, ironically, it was less attractive as the hours were longer but did not pay overtime like regular staff. And becoming a fast-food manager certainly had no links to windsurfing either.

Although most of the managers were pretty decent, there was an exception: a middle-aged Nigerian woman, a shift supervisor who was a control freak and so lacking in any personal warmth whatsoever that she managed to terrorise most of the people around her although she somehow overlooked me. She was a classic case of a little bit of power going straight to a person's head with little or nothing positive coming from it.

My hard work also led to a huge appetite and now and again an extra burger might find its way onto my tray for my break. At the same time, management were dealing with money going missing from the till and the focus had shifted to those working there the longest. I had been caught previously with two burgers in one box by a manager but got away with a mild rebuke, along the lines of 'just don't get caught'. However, management were in the middle of a meeting to discuss the till-thieving as I walked into the staff room on a break with my tray carrying excess allowance.

Seizing the opportunity and knowing that their investigation was common knowledge amongst the staff, I was greeted with 'Come in, Damian, we were just talking about you . . .' It transpired, however, that it was the supervisor from hell who had been dipping the tills, waiting until the end of each shift to cream off a few notes, then adjusting the takings to make it seem that everyone on the front counter was stealing.

The Wimpy experience turned out to be more than just a fast-food job and there were plenty of new lessons for this rather innocent teenager from rural Ireland. Closing time was at night, or really early morning – we shut up shop at 2 a.m. for a few hours of cleaning. One night I was locking the front door after the late shift had arrived when a customer ran up and tried to push past.

'I'm sorry, sir, but we're closed 'til six a.m.,' I said politely.

'Let me in, let me in, open the fucking door,' he roared.

'But we're closed, I'm sorry.'

'Fuck you, Paddy, I'm coming in, you'll fucking see,' and he turned away towards his car where he opened his boot and started rummaging around inside.

My back was up, but luckily, in the next instant my friend Midhat came running from the back of the kitchen, shouting at me to get away from the door. He was an Ethiopian with very long fingernails, suggestive of royal lineage in his homeland, but he was clearly more savvy than I was.

'What's his problem,' I asked. 'Can't he see we're closed?'

'Don't worry about it, just come away from the door,' he implored.

'Sure, what can he do? We're locked inside,' I argued as Midhat steered me firmly to the back kitchen from where we could make out the angry customer lifting some kind of weapon from the boot of the car.

Drugs and guns were another new aspect of life I hadn't seen anything of in Caherdaniel; the country kid badly needed to be more street smart and though Wimpy had its advantages, after nine months of a very limited diet it was time to move on, complete with my full driving licence and a little extra cash.

─◄○►─

The double load of free-sheet newspapers was bound to take a toll sooner or later. Running up and down flights of stairs in Tower Hamlets to avoid the piss and shit in the elevators, even if they were working, was no substitute for proper training.

Each morning we would gather at a corner in Clapham where a van would pull up to issue our supplies. We were each assigned an area and paid according to how many papers we took. Although many people simply ditched their load in the nearest dumpster after making a few token deliveries, checks were made and I was determined that my patch would be properly served. In any case, I would be guilt-ridden if I even threw away even five papers.

After the first week, I had worked out that the high-density blocks of flats were more profitable than a long street of better-off or fewer houses so doubling up the load seemed to make sense. Except that after two months of twin bags swinging around unnaturally from my shoulders, the constant lugging and bending to drop into letterboxes resulted in a crippling hernia condition that would probably not have happened years later in the days of health and safety awareness. It took a National Health Service operation to fix and just a few friends knew about the hospital visit. It was only later on that I realised I had not phoned home to keep them in the picture. I was independent and determined to do everything alone.

There was no going back to the newspaper game. It was the summer of 1987 and my parents had embarked on a major goodwill cruise on the *Canna* to Leningrad, at that time still firmly locked behind the Iron Curtain. So, with a full driving licence and a little pocket money left over, the seas and beaches of Derrynane were calling and it was time to return to Kerry.

Derrynane 1987

Since the summer of 1984, Ossie and Helen Wilson had been building their business steadily and had given Rob, Patrick, Rupert and me summer jobs as water-sports instructors by the beach at Derrynane Harbour. Pat and I concentrated on windsurfing while Rupert did the sailing and Rob looked after the waterskiing. It was the teenage idyll: beach life and sailing by day, free house and parties by night.

When I returned in 1987 the Wilsons had upgraded from the Hiace van to a caravan on the beach: Derrynane Sea Sports was created and has endured the test of time. Ossie's enthusiasm for life and expertise in water sports, plus Helen's persistent encouragement to be open and communicate with people of any age meant they were our natural mentors and we were immersed in the sport all around us. As Laird Hamilton and Robbie Nash blasted down waves and out of the magazine pages, Don Henley's *Boys of Summer* was blasting from the transistor radio in the caravan. That was our base and the centre of beach activities whilst waiting for the wind to blow or girls to walk down the pier. We didn't know it at the time but the adults referred to us as 'The Bleach Boys' for the amount of hydrogen peroxide we were putting in our hair.

The typical day started at 10.30 a.m. with classes at 11 a.m., 2 p.m. and 4 p.m., though later on in the afternoon and on more than one occasion Ossie would become frustrated by our knack of individually blending into the dunes and disappearing.

'Stop fornicating in those fucking sand dunes!' he would roar. 'One of you little bollixes get down here and do some work!'

Ossie and Helen had three children – Alice, Sean and Mark – just a few years younger than us but we all shared the same free spirit passed on from our parents. Helen, in particular, encouraged us to get used to speaking with people of different age groups and not to be shy; this was a natural part of growing up with the different generations in our area.

Fresh with a full driving licence, I thought it would be a good idea to take my father's car for a trial drive at night on home turf. But without his express permission since he was out of contact, it seemed wise to leave the driveway without lights rather than draw the attention of the neighbours. Except that leaving the house meant crossing the cattle grid and taking a sharp left turn onto the narrow lane; without headlights I missed the turn in the pitch dark and the car slid into the ditch on the other side of the road, denting the right-hand panels. That and a smallish dent on a shopping trip to town the following week should have been warning enough but worse was to follow.

With a party in full swing at the house, a friend needed to get home near Lamb's Head on the other side of the village so the car was called into service. I returned to the party later on, to avoid missing too much of the *craic*. However, even with the headlights on but with a little too much speed I took the corner in a skid and managed to drag the car down along a stone wall, eventually stopping in front of the house where everyone had full view of the latest damage.

I had already started feeble attempts to repair the previous damage but this situation was much worse. And to add to the mess, Mum was returning ahead of *Canna* after their successful trip. They had sailed from Derrynane north to Scotland and the Caledonian Canal, across the

North Sea to Norway, then Göteborg on Sweden's west coast, across the Göta Canal to the Baltic city of Helsinki and on to Leningrad. Returning, *Canna* hugged the southern coast, sailing into Estonia, Latvia and Poland before Mum departed for home.

The plan was for me to join the *Canna* in Brighton for the final delivery home to Derrynane. But, when Mum saw the car, her fury seemed set to scupper that plan as she tore strips off me for my shameful breach of their trust. When she calmed down, she said she would not tell my father until after he finished the epic voyage. In fact, she did tell him privately but they decided to say nothing rather than spoil the offshore passage from Brighton via the Scilly Isles. That resolve soon became redundant on our return: the state of his car ignited Dad and though I didn't need another telling off to know I had wrecked the car, I got one anyway. Guilty, as charged.

Portsmouth, England

Once again, the summer was over and there was little option but to journey back to Britain once more, wiser after the previous experience in London but not much more so. With a little money left over from my summer work, I routed through the capital and onwards to Portsmouth to be closer to the sea, though in those days, the Royal Navy port had yet to develop as a sailing centre. Straight away, I found work at the local Wimpy, thanks to good references from the Piccadilly Circus store managers and I found digs at a bedsit near Hayling Island where my neighbour was a building contractor.

Before long, I left the world of burgers and chips for a job as a hoddie on a local building site. It was as unskilled as it was simple work: my duties included wetting the mortar boards and bringing bricks from the delivery pallet on my hod to the scaffold to be easily laid by the bricklayers. Best of all, it paid proper money – £40 per day, just for carrying bricks and cement.

I quickly became fit and strong and before long had saved enough money to buy a windsurfer. After work every day, I would carry the rig down the street to the beach and sailed along the sea front. Although there was a local club, I needed to save money and so fell into a daily routine, even in winter when it got dark before 6 p.m. and seafront lighting was barely sufficient to surf along the waves kicked up by the current running against the banks and groynes just offshore. On top of the daytime workload, which was exhausting, by late evening I would often fall asleep in the bath, happy to be both working and sailing.

Compared to life in London, east Portsmouth was a safer place all round. The gang of lads on the site were a pleasant bunch, all brickies, mostly from Wales and northern England and friendly towards the only Irishman on the site. Although there was very little socialising, their good nature extended to all manner of assistance towards the only 'nipper' in the group.

Within days of starting, I was quickly initiated, being sent on pointless errands to find the boss to request a 'long stand' or to empty the tool store in search of a 'round square'. Aside from the impressive work rate on the site, there were other lessons of a more practical nature, though the best learnt were inevitably of the near-miss variety; 'situational awareness' became a skill born of life-or-death necessity. Shortly after starting the job I was cleaning a cement mixer when a stone got jammed and it was only when my arm was halfway in to free it that I realised with a shock that it could easily restart if the blockage freed itself. Almost a week later, though often warned about walking across scaffold boards with unsecured ends, I was carrying a full hod of bricks when I stepped on a trap on the fourth storey of the building. As I fell, I only just managed to catch a beam in each hand to avoid following the contents of my hod down through the joists of the floors below. (None of the floors had been built so the unimpeded descent to the basement would probably have been fatal.)

In hindsight, these were practical lessons but at the time it was more of a dawning realisation that invincibility is a condition ripe to be tripped up by the unknown and surprised by the unexpected.

Dale, Wales

After six months in Portsmouth, I started flicking through magazines, looking for windsurfing jobs ahead of the new season and did a marine VHF radio course to start adding qualifications. Two jobs, both in Wales on the Pembrokeshire coast, instantly appealed and, after taking the train to attend interviews, I was offered both jobs. One was near Swansea but the other, close to Dale, offered a better course that taught windsurfers how to wave sail. Within a few weeks, I upped sticks and moved to live at the

West Wales Windsurfing Centre, which boasted Britain's best conditions.

Dale was considered a classic windsurfing venue due to the wide range of sailing conditions along a small stretch of coastline that was sheltered from the open Atlantic by a headland at the entrance to the Milford Haven waterway so beginners could learn in safety. It was a familiar environment with wild coastline, farming land and long sandy beaches and felt much like southwest Kerry.

It was a great school, and counted a former British champion amongst the instructors. Dee was a former semi-pro surfer and we would often go sailing late in the evening after the teaching day was over. If we weren't around Broadhaven for wave sailing, we would head directly out past the heads to open water. One weekend we were outside, blasting downwind, until eventually I decided to head back. I signalled to Dee that I was heading in as I was on a promise ashore.

By the time the gear was put away and I had changed at our instructors' chalet close to the beach, there was no sign of Dee. I headed down to the bar overlooking the bay where we were just discussing when Dee might return when someone walked in and said the rescue helicopter had just pulled him from the sea after his mast broke. Much later on, he arrived back and though I half-expected him to be mad at me, he was fairly relaxed – more sheepish than cross. Although we had clearly understood that he was staying out alone, I should have been more concerned much sooner and at least sailed back out to check on him. We were friends but we had yet to understand one another fully after working together for just a few months. The easy-going nature and free spirit of beach culture had its disadvantages as well. Complacency came with a cost.

Leaving Europe and Crossing the Atlantic

Soon the 1988 season would come to a close. By a stroke of good fortune one of the other students from the radio course got in touch about a place on a boat for a delivery from the south coast of England to Portugal and onwards to the Canary Islands. He was bound for the Caribbean and needed sailors for the first stage before his transatlantic crew joined in Gran Canaria.

It seemed too good an opportunity to turn down. As a child I had read many sailing books, such as Dougal Robertson's *Survive the Savage Sea* or various stories by the colourful Tristan Jones and this was finally a chance to try out some deep-sea adventures and travel.

It was a 45-foot cruising boat with just four of us on board: the skipper, his wife, myself and a Kiwi girl called Sandy; both 'couples' split into two watches. It was the longest sea trip I had done and I happily looked forward to sailing across the Bay of Biscay and down the Iberian Peninsula to Vilamoura and on to the Canaries.

Dad had taught me navigation as part of a course for a coastal skipper certificate. From crewing with him on the *Canna*, watch-keeping duties, especially at night, were not new and the trip passed uneventfully. When we reached Puerto Rico in Gran Canaria, the full crew arrived and, as per our agreement, I stepped off the boat, so my private hopes of being invited to remain on for the passage westwards were dashed. The skipper was very good and before they left on the next section of the voyage helped find accommodation for me through the owner of the sail loft.

Life in the Canaries was the polar opposite of living in London and the warm sunshine and mountains were ideal for walking and exploring. While other young people arriving in the islands opted to sell timeshare apartments, I found a job working for a guy called Carlos who owned a tourist bar in a corner of a shopping centre in Puerto Rico. While getting to the Caribbean was now the main objective, it became clear that a defined east-to-west migratory season ran for six months in winter so it was simply a case of waiting for a crewing opportunity to come along.

In the meantime, working for Carlos became a mixture of learning the bar trade and Spanish at once, in a flashy Frank-Sinatra-themed setting. It was a period of struggle, of making ends meet on minimum bar earnings based on a six-day week starting at 4 p.m. and finishing at 3 a.m. There was certainly insufficient spare cash to go windsurfing and a return trip home for Christmas was definitely out of the question too. My Spanish improved, thanks to the local clientele, as did my expertise in making cocktails, while a professional waiter taught me how to carry a heavily laden tray of drinks through a crowded bar, perched on three fingers, without spilling a drop. Under careful instruction from Carlos, the trick of upping the bar tabs of unsuspecting customers was revealed, usually at the expense of drunk Scandinavians. In turn, we never quite received the share of tips he collected; basically, we were working for a right bollix. It was a hand-to-mouth existence but my day off was a chance to walk in the mountains or hang out at the beach and maybe meet girls. I learnt how to say good night and good morning in Finnish and was glad not to be selling timeshares.

It was possible to wander around the dock and meet people coming and going on boats, usually westward bound, and I was invited on board one boat to watch a home movie of the previous year's transatlantic passage. More than ever, it was time to get going: the Caribbean was the place to be. I had always been vaguely aware that a circuit of sorts existed there and it would be a good place to live. More importantly, I also realised that the crossing needed to be made before hurricane season started at the end of May or face being trapped in the Canaries during the peak summer months. Carlos protested when he learned I would be leaving before the spring or as soon as an offer on a boat came up. He dismissed my ideas as fanciful but I was determined and anyway, by that stage, I had had enough of Carlos.

So, on another day off on a trip to Puerto Mogan on the south end of the island, I was standing on the quay wall when a sleek, white-hulled maxi racing yacht sailed up to the harbour, dropped sails and motored to a berth inside.

As the boat came closer, distinct Irish accents could be heard amongst others: American, Kiwi and British. Closer still, in large letters surrounded by a Celtic motif, the words *NCB Ireland*.

It was late January 1989 and the 82-foot yacht was Ireland's first-ever entry for the Whitbread Round-the-

World Race that started in November of that year. The 24-strong crew was en route to its winter training ground for practice and team selection at the Maxi World Championship at St Thomas in the US Virgin Islands.

I had not heard anything about the boat before and was overwhelmed with shyness by its size and the professional manner of its crew. It might have been better had I presented myself with a little confidence – perhaps there might have been a role for a nipper while in port (a berth on board for the crossing was a non-starter). But I kept my distance and *NCB Ireland* sailed on to the Caribbean and the path to a professional sailing career remained obscured.

It was not until the spring, almost at the end of the season, that a lucky break happened on a day spent pounding the dock looking for a berth. The twentieth boat turned out to belong to a French sailor who with his wife was making the crossing on their 38-foot cruising catamaran named *Log*. Their three-year-old daughter was suffering from seasickness and another hand was needed on board.

Carlos was at last given his due notice and a happy month followed, preparing *Log* for the transatlantic trip, servicing winches, checking the rigging and loading food bags. It was an important exercise and the contrast between the impersonal streets of London and of walking down this dock, people trusting and open enough to allow you to share a boat with no escape for weeks on end, was not lost on me. (Try the same thing on land – walk into any stranger's house and asking for a bed and water for the night – and you would not get a more opposite response.)

Eventually, fresh water was last to be topped up before we quietly slipped away from Gran Canaria. Once under way, we picked up the trade winds almost immediately and the four of us settled into the routine that would keep us busy for the next month and 2,700 miles of fast sailing to Antigua. It felt very natural to be at sea, normal even, and despite the scale of the great Atlantic Ocean, it was not an intimidating place. Habits were easily formed on board. What might pass for monotony became all the more remarkable as subtle changes in weather, cloud formations, temperature, sea state, wind strength and more all took on added meanings and importance. Our boat was more than a home: it was a survival craft, hundreds of miles from assistance where self-reliance became an invaluable currency. Hours on watch, time off watch, rest, food and maintaining *Log* became so systematic that time fused, days into weeks, until civilisation beckoned once more.

Our landfall was at dusk on a Sunday night and reggae sounds from a traditional steel band party carried over the gentle evening breeze from the old Nelson lookout post on Shirley Heights overlooking English and Falmouth Harbours. We could not have asked for a better fanfare as we sailed almost silently past the headland until *Log* lay to anchor in a cove surrounded by mangrove, which gave way to a beach backed with coconut palms and tamarind trees. The smell of the island and the sounds ashore spoke of exotic new places to explore. This was my introduction to the place I was to call home for the next six years.

5

Sun, Sand, Sea and Sailing

Somewhere Between St Barths and St Martin

As the yelling match between the husband and wife got louder and more intense, the other guests moved as far away from the pair as was possible on a 70-foot catamaran while they traded insults. Fuelled by too much sun and far too much rum punch, it was not such an uncommon scene on our daily 15-mile sail from St Martin to St Barths, though this fight was particularly spite-filled.

Our morning departure from Philipsburg was routine enough and, though I was on board this boat as stand-in for another regular crew member, the small fleet of similarly sized cruising cats that carried tourists for day trips was like an extended family and we all mixed easily. The row had started during the extended lunch stop on St Barths. The longer upwind haul, bashing into the short seas in the freshening daily breeze, left the guests on the island for five hours before our return sail, which was always a brisk

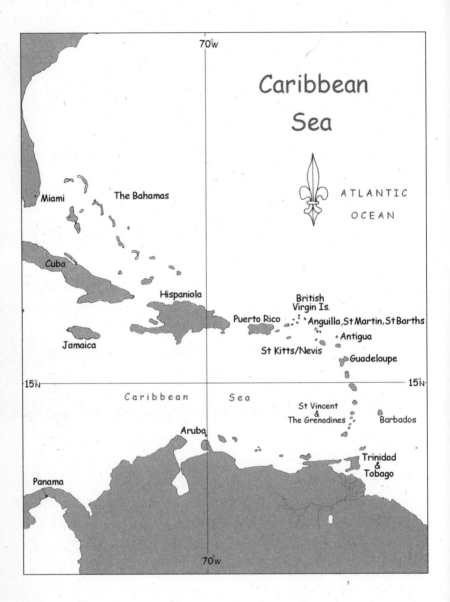

sprint downwind under spinnaker. Neither the crew nor any of the other twenty guests actually knew what the argument was about except that it was ruining a perfectly lovely day out sailing.

'You're a goddamned liar,' she roared. 'I hate you and I wish I'd never met you!'

'Screw you, bitch. Nobody forced you to marry me,' he returned. 'If I could get away from you right now, I would.'

'Go on then, go . . .'

'Maybe I just might, d'ya think I can't?'

'I couldn't give a shit if you drown right here and now!'

With that he marched across the trampoline netting between the hulls, his drunken gait masked by the slight heave of the boat as it sped downwind at close to 20 knots. As the other guests looked on in amazement, he lurched over the guardrail and reappeared seconds later in our wake with a look of bewilderment at his own action and no doubt sobered by the cool seawater.

Instantly, the skipper yelled 'man overboard' and spun the wheel, barely giving us time to blow the spinnaker halyard and rush forward to gather the sail hastily into an untidy mess on the trampoline. Within five minutes, we were back alongside the man who was sheepishly treading water as he awaited rescue, unaware of how close he might have been to death had he been knocked unconscious in the fall overboard. Using a boathook, we steered him alongside the hull and aft to the swimming ladder, which was dropped down.

After he was hauled back on deck and with his now concerned wife by his side, the skipper came over to check him out. He was a tough, leather-skinned, hard-drinking Aussie and could easily have been Crocodile Dundee's older, slightly heavier brother: not the type to suffer fools gladly.

'I'm okay, I'm fine,' whined the dripping swimmer.

'Are you sure?' asked the skipper.

'Yup, no problem. Justa lil' swim to cool down,' he said drily, whereupon the skipper delivered a sudden uppercut to his jaw, knocking the passenger backwards onto the trampoline where he bounced around before his wife went to his aid.

'Don't ever fucking do that on my boat or any boat ever again,' growled the skipper. The other passengers nodded their silent appreciation and the crew turned away to hide their grim smiles.

We didn't bother with the spinnaker again as we were close to Philipsburg and a large windless zone in the lee of the island would have stopped us anyway. We motored to the dock and said farewell to the guests. It had otherwise been an uneventful day and though unusual to have had a skipper deck a paying passenger, it had to be taken as part of the variety that life in the Caribbean brought at a time when mass tourism was still in its infancy.

Caribbean

Laying claim to 'paradise' status seems to be a regular occurrence just about anywhere in the world that has something special to offer. It does not have to mean sun and palm trees, though for many people this is exactly what they expect paradise to be. Apparently, estate agents and holiday sales reps are especially prone to this vision. By coincidence, in Irish mythology, *Tír na nÓg* – the land of youth – is said to lie far out to sea, west of Ireland, in a place that can be reached only after an arduous voyage. And in keeping with all the classic paradises, it is a place where music, strength, food, drink and life are everlasting. As it happens, the Caribbean lies somewhat west of Ireland and if paradise is indeed a place of eternal happiness, where life and all pleasurable pursuits come together, then the West Indies must surely be just such a place.

Yet, despite the modern idyll, the 7,000-plus islands of the region were far from being Utopia and achieved notoriety up to the nineteenth century as a plundered colony and slave-trade haven that indelibly stamped the territories with a marque that is clear to this day. Less well known is that Irish prisoners were counted amongst those manacled travellers and for them, white sandy beaches and trade winds were pitiful recompense for enforced labour, removal from their families and homes. Only recently has a semblance of economic independence arrived, most of it utterly reliant on the region's tourist appeal and its paradise moniker. And as during its colonial past, sailing features strongly within these island nations as old and new worlds collide, often with apparent ease.

It was into this new order that *Log* had deposited me after our transatlantic journey, first to Antigua but soon after to Saint Maarten/Saint Martin, the Dutch/French dependency further northwest in the Lesser Antillean chain of small islands that stands on the Atlantic side of the Caribbean Sea. On arrival there, after our farewells in

Marigot, the bustling main town of the French side, I hitched around the island at the start of a new adventure. In Grand Casse, a small quiet traditional village on the north of the island, Marla at the Wave Restaurant suggested a visit to the local dock at Philipsburg, the capital of the Dutch side and centre of the day charter business. That advice instantly landed me a job that was as near to the dream assignment as any boat-mad nineteen-year-old might ask for.

The job was with a small fleet of catamarans, the biggest of which was *Eagle* at 70-feet overall and beautifully built in cold-moulded plywood in the Brookes yard on St Kitts. She was laid out specifically for carrying tourists on sailing day trips between the islands and, best of all, the job was live-aboard and came with a daily wage of US$40 plus whatever tips were going. *Eagle* would become home for the next three years though with regular interruptions to fill in on other boats such as *El Tigre* or *Falcon*, both sailing catamarans.

Each day, we would leave St Martin and sail to either St Barths or Anguilla, both idyllic, remote destinations with anywhere from five to twenty passengers, sometimes in company with *Falcon*, another 70-footer that we would race semi-seriously and more so if a round of beers in the bar that evening was at stake. The morning stage of the day would be spent banging upwind for around 15 miles and, as the daily trade winds freshened, so too did the sea state pick up. One skipper and two of us crew would run the boat while also serving the guests with Heinekens and rum punch. Most lasted the journey without being seasick but there were occasional chronic cases, which made the trips more arduous for all.

On arrival, the visitors had a long lunch break, sampling local dishes such as chicken in peas and rice with johnny cakes, a type of cornmeal bread. More often, the guests opted for liquid refreshments. The three-hour break gave us time off and the local restaurants and car-hire companies sometimes looked after us as a thank-you for bringing customers their way, so the middle of the day became a free and easy way to see the islands, provided the maintenance work on the boat was up to date. Later in the afternoon, the guests would return for the fast downwind sprint back to Philipsburg under the giant masthead spinnaker that was the headline act for crew and passengers alike.

It was a simple, happy-go-lucky lifestyle and I had not a care in the world. In many respects the Caribbean felt like Kerry – regional, traditional, tolerant – and I felt perfectly at home. After work or after play, a few beers in the evening were standard and, not unusually for a holiday resort, there were always a few people at the bar first who were last to leave. It is somewhat harder in the Caribbean, though. Somehow the beer is cooler, the sun is hotter and the company almost always appears more attractive. For a teenager without definite plans beyond a few months and with a $40-a-day job on a catamaran (which seemed always to end up paying a bar bill each week), this was the extent of my serious ambition; life was good.

It was a point of personal pride to take the job seriously and work hard. Despite this, it gradually became clear that a plan was needed. There was little point not having any goals and simply going with the wind if achieving your full potential was supposed to be the outcome. As a result, and though initially the heavy-drinking lifestyle was fun, it ultimately held little long-term interest. After a long period of eating-sleeping-sailing-drinking-sailing, the novelty of the daily bar routine wore thin and I was conscious that others were spending more and more time in the bars socialising while I wanted to do other things.

That choice began when we came ashore after the end of the Guavaberry Series 60-mile race from St Martin to St Kitts. A big party ashore was held on the back of the beach under the coconut palms with a live, local reggae band and rum 'n' cokes going down well. Late in the evening as I was getting another round in, my friends John-Paul and Miriam untypically refused another beer as they were planning to compete in a swimming race the following morning.

I should have known they were athletes – broad shoulders and very fit – but the idea of competition grabbed my attention, especially as it was not a straightforward race. It was a 3-mile sprint across the narrows between Majors Bay on St Kitts and the Oualie Beach Resort on neighbouring Nevis and a strong current generated by the trade winds blowing between the two high volcanic islands added to the challenge. I had more than a few beers that night, but walking down the beach at 7.00 a.m. to join the boatload of swimmers, Jean-Paul passed me a bottle of water and the haze and beginnings of a mild headache gave way to what would become a familiar feeling: the rush of adrenalin. I began swimming and running in my time off in the middle of the day, skipping long midday lunches and beers and quickly became friends with a group who were training for triathlons, and who welcomed this newcomer even if he couldn't afford a competition bike.

Before long, within a few months, a daily rhythm emerged of sailing and living on board *Eagle* by day, training with friends in the evenings and parties at weekends mostly; and all the time, learning the trade of looking after boats and meeting people with different stories of the world of sailing as they visited the islands. It was almost as if the Windward Islands were a permanent grandstand for the succession of transoceanic races such as the Route du Rhum, Transat Jacques Vabre and other short-handed competitions that invariably seemed to be completely French-dominated if not French-inspired. Clearly, France was a significant centre of deep-sea sailing.

From my earliest days of living in the Caribbean, I could tell from which island a person came – Dominica, Puerto Rico, Haiti, St Kitts especially – from the way they looked or spoke, regardless of whether they were black, white or brown. Strong cultural differences ran through the different islands. Though it is never good to stereotype, it was clear that St Vincent had the bluntness of Nigeria whereas in the south end of the Caribbean chain, Grenada and Trinidad were more like Ghana or Senegal where the people are gentle and easy going. The murder rate on St Thomas was on a par with Chicago so we avoided the main centre, Charlotte Amalie, and stayed in Red Hook on the opposite side of the island, away from the potentially hostile streets. Montserrat, Saba and Nevis were like any rural community where you could securely walk down the road in the middle of the night.

Antigua had smaller problems, mostly hinged around anti-colonial issues amongst younger people. Actually, to be fair, there was a bit of that in most islands and, though the

French and Dutch islands were the most liberal, the result of the old traditional race and class divides lingered on in all the former colonies. But generally, in most of the islands a relaxed and friendly atmosphere was the result of a good lifestyle and a positive tourism industry.

Whether native or newcomer, everyone entered into the culture of the islands where the highlight of the Caribbean year is carnival. Each island has its own format that becomes a mini-industry although it manages to stay low key in contrast to the hype of somewhere like Rio de Janeiro. On St Martin, you simply could not get fired if you didn't turn up for work during Carnival week. The warm-up and rehearsals – J'Ouvert morning – for the show ahead would begin at 4 a.m. with a stop for breakfast at 7 a.m. By midday, everyone would be ready for the parade and opening ceremony. It was impossible to escape the celebration and with sounds of calypso, salsa and reggae music everywhere, the parade brought the trucks of bands and speakers booming down the street, dancers of different groups in fabulous dress, swaying in bikinis and less, glistening under the sun. Food was plentiful and chicken wings, corn cobs and spare ribs would be served from oil-drum barbeques at the side of the road. We would sail the boats to St Kitts and Nevis where their carnivals were always the most fun – the locals' attitude and openness made the difference.

Summer was not as pleasant and was often boring with fewer visitors though the calmer seasonal waters were better for diving. The end of that season was welcome and invariably marked by huge rainstorms that would soak the earth and feed the forests so their dry foliage would light up in brilliant radiance. The humidity would dry up and the air became clearer so the islands looked their very best. The autumn rains fed the salt ponds, which were mosquito-infested and best to be avoided, not least for their smell.

Autumn was always pleasant as the trade winds would return, bringing much-needed relief from the intense summer heat. At last, we could sail again instead of constantly motoring around. The winter brought stronger and stronger winds so that by December we would have a good 25 knots each day. With deep blue skies, almost guaranteed wind and unspoilt waters, it was truly heaven on earth and the best of all worlds. At Christmas, most homes had a decorated tree and houses and shacks would be covered in American-style lights. If you didn't have a house, a tamarind tree would be decorated instead.

Winter was peak tourist season for visitors from North America and Europe who were escaping from shivering in the seasonal weather that I was all too familiar with from living in Kerry. Our daily pattern of taking groups of visitors sailing around the nearby islands continued until spring when the trades disappeared once more to make way for hurricane season from June onwards. These tropical storms occur when the Atlantic becomes warmer and reaches 19.4 degrees Celsius. Huge heat energy is released from the ocean into the atmosphere where it spins up into a vicious pattern of destructive and potentially fatal high winds that drive storm surges, flatten buildings and catch the least prepared, usually the poorest inhabitants, off guard with tragic consequences.

Luckily, since I arrived in St Martin in the spring of 1989, the worst storms such as Hurricane Hugo had passed, though plenty more threatened and battening down the hatches was a regular if unwelcome occurrence – we were paid only for the days we sailed. None of us could afford not to work or even be sick, and travel insurance was not an option, nor health insurance, as we were all working illegally, though a blind eye was turned.

As the peak season neared its end, we used to race the boats in the annual Heineken Regatta. There was also a regular evening race series and I started crewing with my South African friend, Duncan Ross, on a Prindle 19, a small-class racing catamaran dinghy similar to the Olympic Tornado. There was even a competitive racing circuit around the islands, for which I was usually allowed time off work to race.

Virgin Islands

For the biggest series, the Caribbean Offshore Racing Triangle (CORT) series,we left St Martin to sail the 120 miles offshore to the Virgin Islands. Five boats left in the brisk 25-knot trades and we were joined by a large yacht that was on delivery but also served as our mother ship. Our small fleet comprised various levels of ability, including a Frenchman and his girlfriend who were barely more than beginners.

Our 'race' northwards got under way but after a few hours of hard reaching, the French couple capsized in the huge seas. We all abandoned our passage race to stand by them and assist in righting their boat. But it was no use: their cat had turned over completely and the seaway was making matters worse. Eventually, Duncan jumped in along with another sailor from one of the other competent cats and had to unpin the rig so that the boat could be righted. Meanwhile, I sailed our boat single-handed, circling the scene and keeping in contact with the other boats as the big waves sloshed over the trampoline. The mother ship eventually caught up and took the couple on board before taking their dismasted boat in tow. As it was now late in the afternoon, with no land in sight and still a way to go, a debate followed about whether to press on to the BVIs. Duncan and I decided to sail on without the others and after a few more hours we reached The Baths, Virgin Gorda, just before nightfall at the end of our trip.

The following morning, the mother ship arrived, now with two boats in tow and minus a third that was lost overnight when it went up on rocks. But it was a minor incident in which nobody died or was injured and for the next six weeks we raced at different venues for short, three-day regattas. Between events, we would have a few days in hand to reach the next destination in the CORT series so we island-hopped in our beach cats, sailing by day and pulled up on sheltered and isolated beaches each evening. We fished and made open fires, sometimes slept in tents but more often under the stars. We beached on Jost Van Dyke and visited Foxy's Bar, then and now a Caribbean legend, and went climbing and diving on the outlying islands in the channel and discovered some of the most beautiful dive locations of anywhere in the world.

The small boats were ideal for exploring the places like the fabulous reef islands, such as Vieques and Culebra close to Puerto Rico or Anegada near the BVI comprised of low, flat sand and coral with the outlying reefs protecting extensive lagoons of fish, turtles and not a person in sight. Lacking airports and direct flights, these islands are only accessible by sea. St Martin with direct flights from the US and Europe got a head-start on the rest of the region with mass tourism, which relied on convenience, and few people bothered exploring the more distant islands. Their loss was our gain with our sailing equivalent to the backpackers' lifestyle.

But if our 'raiding' around the islands was an adventure, Duncan brought it to new levels a few years later when he began an expedition to 'join' the tropics of Cancer and Capricorn. The 6,000-mile expedition linked Florida to Recife in Brazil and involved motor-sailing beach cats up the Orinoco Delta in Venezuela, as far as the upper rainforests, spending three weeks there before linking to the Amazon and exiting at the river delta and into the Atlantic. In company with the second cat, he had to sail upwind in 25 knots for 1,000 miles and, along the way, one boat broke its mast threatening to end the fifty-day expedition. The other boat had to leave the second cat and its two crew on the outlying sandbar and sail/trek for three days to the nearest town across sandbanks, mudflats and rainforest to find spare parts, leaving the two castaways in the middle of the Amazon delta, running out of food and hoping they would make it back. This kicked off a list of major exploits for him culminating in what will remain as an extreme benchmark for all, the crossing from Cape Horn across the Drake Passage to the ice-strewn Antarctic Peninsula, once again on a beach cat.

—◦—

At that time, it seemed that life could not be better. I had no fixed sporting objectives and was still growing up, happily living life as it happened. A dream emerged, a bucket list, of living on a shack by a beach with a laundry line out the back and a reef just offshore to row out to (not motor) and fish some pots. Just like the older people at home in Kerry, here too in the Caribbean people were living the simple life. I had not yet fully decided what to do with my own life but I could see how I would like to finish up my years. Whether in the Caribbean or Kerry, it doesn't matter: the need for a simple life in a complicated world is ever present. It was as carefree a lifestyle as anyone might ask for, working hard at the job and training hard for both sport and fitness.

House-minding

Nevertheless, it could be an awkwardly steep learning curve at times. The skipper of *Style*, a Saba diving boat, was away for a week and asked me to look after things for him while he was gone. The invitation included living in his house – a very nice house – and as I had been living afloat for three years, it was too good an opportunity to turn down. With full cable TV and plenty of missed movies to catch up on, I settled in on his huge, comfy sofa to watch *Die Hard 1* and *2*.

While loading up on snacks in the back room, I also discovered a Very pistol, normally used for firing distress flares at sea but left in the house for home protection. Unfortunately for *Saba*'s skipper, it became a prop for my enthusiasm for the shoot-outs on TV. Except I didn't realise that it was loaded and at the first opportunity to return fire, the red flare erupted from the muzzle and shot around the room, bounced off the walls a few times and buried itself into the sofa that I had managed to abandon barely a millisecond earlier. The lovely couch ignited and only by stuffing cushions onto the flames could I extinguish the mini-inferno. Eventually there was little to tell between the TV show and the living room; shoot-outs had occurred in both.

It was a setback of sorts, not just in terms of the embarrassment of letting down the owner but also myself. And then one day, not long after the Very pistol incident, *Eagle*'s owner Evie, who gave me my first job in Philipsburg, asked me to take over as skipper of her boat: a second reason why I'll be grateful to her for the rest of my life. It would be a totally new challenge with a new level of expectation of me, by me and by others.

New Role as Skipper

Taking on the role of a skipper means discovering new skills such as communication, calmness under pressure as well as seamanship and experience so that this inspires confidence and loyalty. Sincerity in recognising the limitations of boat and crew and not necessarily being the most experienced on board is the only certain way to develop in the role plus avoiding the absolute 'no-no' of blaming or shouting at the crew when things go wrong.

Although the job was very familiar and the routine came naturally, the most difficult part of skippering was docking the big cats with just one outboard engine – it was something of a credibility issue, as it is for most boats. It is the one moment when everyone has nothing to do but watch and wait for you to get it right or get it wrong. Plain and simple. A narrow space, the breeze pushing you the wrong way, too much engine power and you can crash into the dock; or worse, too little power and you will crash into the neighbouring boat.

Most people in the industry knew Steve whose old wooden sloop was as beautiful as his girlfriend and he offered a chartering service in the area. It was not unusual to give lifts to our friends if, say, they had left their boat on one island to take a flight home or pick up spare parts from another. One day, Steve asked for a lift to St Barths on our usual run on *Eagle* from Philipsburg, to rejoin his own boat. On our return that evening, the police were waiting on the dockside to take my crew and me to the local jail to answer some questions. The crew was released almost immediately but as skipper I found myself sitting in a cell, extremely nervous and surrounded by crowds of illegal immigrants awaiting deportation to Dominica and Haiti. Our own status was still illegal on the island, even if tolerated by the authorities in the name of developing their tourism industry.

The questioning was to the point: what did I know about Steve? My head was spinning as I tried to figure out what could be wrong. It was just a simple favour, dropping off a pal to a nearby island, a professional courtesy even. Completely normal, no unusual behaviour or dodgy packages. Back in the cell, I had not given them anything useful but only because I had nothing to say other than the simple facts of the day. Deportation loomed as the night wore on until Evie arrived at the gaol and secured my release. Sailing brought good revenues to the island and Evie was well regarded in the community.

Much later, we got word that Steve had been arrested in St Barths where the local police threw him in a cell to await the arrival of Metropol officers from Guadaloupe. It appeared that in the distant past he had been connected to a drugs deal that went bad and someone had been killed. But before the investigators arrived in Gustavia, somehow the key to the cell got left in the lock so Steve managed to walk out and was never seen again.

Despite the circumstances, Steve's absence was accepted as normal, as if he had departed on a long cruise or had simply been around as part of a long stopover. We never found out the full story of what happened but we missed him and were happy that he had escaped. The incident was a reminder that, between tourists and temporary workers, the islands often seemed like bus stations with people coming and going or simply hanging around waiting for their next journey to begin.

In spite of this, all of us had strong links to our own homes, no matter how distant. Yet in six years, I hardly met any Irish people until one day in Chesterfields, a regular after-work bar and restaurant that was the hub of waterfront life, I met Father Pat who was on holiday. The conversation flowed with him as we talked about everything from happenings in Ireland to life on our smaller island. There was a warmth about our chat – he wasn't preachy or out to change me and that reminded me of home. I realised that I underestimated the importance of networking. It was as if I always had do it alone, do it my own way, as if there was something to prove and that state of mind stayed with me, perhaps to make it harder and so make the end result all the more of an achievement.

It meant I didn't phone home very often and while I had occasionally visited my aunt in London when working there, I never asked my relatives or friends for help as instinct drove the desire to be independent. At the time, it had not occurred to me that it would have been to go against the grain not to be self-reliant. It was not that I took home for granted or rejected it and my family. It is just that home is an eternal thing that can never be changed. When you grow up in a place like Bunavalla, it is permanent. That is where I'm from and where I grew up: you can cut a branch off a tree and carry it to the other side of the field but that branch will always be from that tree. It's that simple.

It was 1992 at this point and perhaps I mentioned to Father Pat that I had not been home in four years but he took my address and, without being asked, when he returned to Ireland he wrote to my parents to tell them he had met me, that I was happy and well and had plans. It was a simple yet wonderfully genuine act.

The following year, my parents flew to nearby Montserrat to stay with friends and I joined them there for two weeks. Known as 'the Emerald Isle of the Caribbean', Montserrat had a dormant volcano and the high-sided island was covered in lush rainforest and lost sugar cane plantations with their conical mills now overgrown and abandoned. A historic link to Ireland had been established in 1632 when

Irish Catholic indentured slaves moved there, having been persecuted in neighbouring Nevis. A failed slave uprising in 1768 led to the celebration of St Patrick's Day and following the abolition of slavery in 1834, many of the black slaves took Irish names. We explored the island with its cliffs and the Soufrière Hills volcano, and sailed and swam in the turquoise waters off beaches that might have rivalled Derrynane. Except the palm trees would not have been a match for an Irish winter. Otherwise it could easily have been any family holiday from a few years earlier: nothing had changed and why should it?

Just three years later, after lying dormant for centuries, Montserrat's volcano erupted. The capital town of Plymouth, the airport and harbour were buried under 12 metres of mud. The lava also destroyed the airport and docking facilities, leaving the southern half of the island uninhabitable and caused many people to leave their small island home. The volcano was to remain active for years and at night it was possible to see the glow as dramatic eruptions sent pyroclastic fragments down the sides of the mountain.

Shortly after my parents returned home from the Caribbean, Rupert came out to St Martin for six months of work. He was match-racing on the former America's Cup 12-metre yachts and we lived together in St Petersburg. It had been four years since I had seen him and the young brother that I had left behind in Bunavalla was now a young man. At the end of the season he sailed back to Europe on a delivery trip. I missed him, my family and the *craic* back in Kerry, things I had mostly managed to ignore until then. Suddenly, I realised I had not been home in five years.

Moving On

There was only so much experience to be gained from skippering a 70-foot pleasure catamaran. I did not suffer from delusions of grandeur, especially when the constant stream of professionally managed and crewed racing boats visiting the islands was so tempting to the ambitious eye.

Shag Morton of FKG Rigging in St Martin was something of a living legend in ocean racing and he seemed an obvious starting point. Except that timing is everything and picking Saturday night in a marina bar when he's out with his mates definitely counts as 'the wrong moment'. Instead, I should have waited until first thing on a Monday morning to make an initial approach for a strong first impression. It earned an offhand comment, which was fair enough given the context.

'Be smart about it, get your thoughts together, have a strategy, don't waste his time, make an impression by getting it right – not by approaching him having a beer with his mates in the bar on a Saturday night,' I lectured myself afterwards.

A more reasonable approach – at his workshops at 9.00 a.m. on the Monday morning – was far more productive and he offered plenty of useful advice and some reality checks as well. Breaking into the professional racing scene would be a hard slog involving steadily working up the ranks from being the nipper carrying out the most menial tasks to eventually more responsible roles.

Until this point, life on St Martin had become a steady routine of skippering by day, training in the evenings and racing at weekends. But stepping up a level, even to the most junior function in a professional team, would mean reappraisal and flexibility to respond to opportunities as they arose. Getting started meant going north so when *Donnybrook* stopped off in St Barths, a chance vacancy on the crew meant an opportunity to be introduced into the racing circuit in the United States. She was a ULDB 70-footer – ultra-light displacement boat, a sled basically – owned by Irish American Jim Muldoon and based in Annapolis, Maryland. It was a great opportunity to be introduced to a well-known boat that had an extensive programme of races each year around America and the Caribbean. A week later, after saying my goodbyes and handing in my notice to Evie, we slipped out of Marigot Bay for Florida.

That introduction/delivery turned into a permanent place on the crew for the Pineapple Cup, a race from Miami to Montego Bay via the famed Windward Passage. After that, the boat was shipped to Spain and another invitation followed to rejoin the boat for the Route of Discovery Race that follows Columbus' path. My first transatlantic race, with racing yachts and tall ships thronging the starting line, *Donnybrook* sprinted for the course alongside the massive four-masted Russian steel barque *Sedov*, which unfurled her sails at 20 seconds to go as we thundered to the line in a beautifully timed and spectacular run.

Our next stop was the Canary Islands, briefly, before continuing to Puerto Rico. The return to the islands also marked a complete Atlantic circuit for me from a few years earlier on the much smaller *Log*. From rookie to beach cats, then a 70-foot cat skipper back to nipper on a 70-foot racing yacht. It might have seemed mixed up but every boat was an opportunity to learn and gain experience. Crews raced against rival crews at sea but once ashore, all were equals once more and friendships were formed as stories were exchanged from the long periods at sea. Contacts were made and offers of crew places – as nipper – followed. It was important to keep rolling, keep learning, staying current and a very nomadic period brought a breath of fresh air and energy.

Many of the maxi yachts, boats of around 80 feet LOA (length overall) were preparing for the Whitbread Round-the-World Race and so were closed shops but previous entries were still competing on the rest of the circuit. After sailing on *Donnybrook* from Puerto Rico to New York, an offer of a full-time job on Muldoon's team was made but there were more tempting opportunities and I moved on: a race with the American maxi *Congere* to Boston and then a delivery place on *La Poste*, a French maxi preparing for the passage to Quebec, both getting ready for the Whitbread race. Once in Canada, a place became available on the ex-*UBS Switzerland*, winner of the 1985–1986 Whitbread race for the classic Quebec–Saint-Malo race. It was a very international crew with a largely Slavic and Italian contingent. After successfully completing the transatlantic journey, on arrival in the south of France, we bade farewell to some of our mates who, in stark contrast to the rest of us, were returning to Serbia, Croatia and Montenegro where they were about to go to war.

From the Riviera, a delivery back to the Caribbean completed another full transatlantic circuit. Sea miles, the industry gauge of experience, were being accumulated and I soon had exceeded 25,000 nautical miles. At this stage, ocean racing – especially the Whitbread race – was alluring.

After months away from the Caribbean, my eyes had been opened to a world of new opportunities yet even then, unless permanently working with one boat as a travelling, full-time crew member, there could be long gaps between places for races or deliveries. I started working for Simon Manly's company, Sun Yacht Charters, which would later become part of the much larger Moorings group. The role was as charter skipper, an altogether different job from looking after day-trip tourists. In this new job, clients would arrive to take a boat for a week or two but had little or no experience or simply lacked a cruising plan. The guests would ask for ideas and so we would sail away to many of my favourite places around the islands; to a reggae concert in Antigua, a beach at Jost Van Dyke or perhaps a festival in Anguilla. I would skipper the boat and sometimes we would have a cook join us. Other times, the charter company might need a boat returned from another island so I would do this single-handed as it was usually not more than a day or two at sea. By the time I was twenty-four, I had crossed the Atlantic five times, twice as skipper and twice racing, so the route was starting to become very familiar.

Racing for a Living

Boats are normally run on behalf of an owner by a manager and a boat captain with perhaps a nipper or two, generally as full-time positions. Racing crew positions are more mercenary and include bowman, mastman, pitman, trimmer, driver, navigator, tactician and navigator. Nipper and bowman are two traditional entry points that lead to more involvement and experience and both are suited to younger and often fitter sailors. As part of the typical campaign, crew would be flown to the venue, fed, watered, housed and clothed, usually to a modest or comfortable standard by the owner and in some exceptional cases to the same level of comfort and luxury that the owner would enjoy.

At that time, being young, free and single, I was able to eat, sleep and drink sailing so balancing a relationship or even family commitments with work were not issues that I understood.

In the modern era, it is commonplace for professional crews to have a travel allowance instead of limitless expenses in order to be more family friendly, particularly for older crew members trying to maintain a work/life balance. But it was not always so well understood, especially in the early days of modern professional racing. One skipper got thoroughly frustrated after receiving his umpteenth complaint from a crew wife – matched by a clearly grumpy crewman who was clearly under domestic pressure – that someone else had a nicer apartment. The skipper had had enough so he called all the wives and partners to a meeting that proved very short.

'Ladies, this is our job,' he began. 'We are all here for one thing and one thing only – to win a race, that's all.'

All eyes in the room stared back in curious anticipation of what could be coming next.

'We've invited you here as a courtesy, to make it more comfortable for all the families; but if there are any further issues then we'll end this facility and send the sailors home when they've finished their work – in six months' time.'

Stunned silence greeted the news.

However, the story crucially misses the other side of family life and the sacrifices made by sailing families left ashore to endure the difficulties of the nomadic lifestyle.

It became a cycle: work on the charter boats, break and fly to join the racing team and then back again, home to St Martin for what proved to be a steady stream of income and a living wage. At one end of the spectrum, visitors would fly to our tropical island and become sailors for a relaxing holiday; at the other, wealthy individual owners would fly us sailors to other locations to help them achieve their sporting ambitions.

Both charter and racing boats tended to be around 40 to 70 feet in length though the super-exotic maxi yachts were much bigger at 80 to 100 feet and were much rarer. And though there were few Irish visitors to the Caribbean, competing with the Irish Admiral's Cup *Team Jameson* in 1993 opened more doors for me: to Tom Roche's Mumm 36-footer for a series of regattas that included that class's world championship, the now-defunct Kenwood Cup in Hawaii and the famous San Francisco Big Boat series. Through these campaigns, I met Gordon Maguire from Howth in Dublin, a firmly established professional sailor, and Neal McDonald, a top skiff sailor and professional, as well as Steve Hayles, an up-and-coming navigator, with whom I formed strong friendships.

It was a process that would bring the Caribbean experience to its natural conclusion: a period ending with much greater self-knowledge and belief, of ability, fitness and awareness after a gradual progression from teenager to young adult, and the discovery of potential.

If, years before on the bus from Tralee, there had been a conscious or deliberate decision to set a personal test, then that rite of passage had ended with the satisfaction of survival. It had not been the 'silver-spoon' route, though anyone who has that option should take it. Another option might have been to do an engineering degree and gather intelligence and experience that way. The outcome is what counts and making skipper was recognition only of ability, not of ego.

There was still plenty more to be done and the transoceanic sailors such as Florence Arthaud, sailing her 60-foot trimaran into St Barths – single-handed – had made a huge impact on me. It seemed like a contrast but it was more like a full circle of sorts. Barely five years earlier, life revolved around the beach, sailing, adventures and friends; little else mattered. Now the whole effort had stepped up more than a few gears and clear opportunities were apparent.

Rupert was studying at university in Britain and, with the family dispersed, *Canna* was sold and my parents were busy with Voluntary Service Overseas and the Agency for Personal Service Overseas and were planning to teach English in China.

On 22 April 1994, I received a call from my father at home in Kerry that was to change our lives forever. A gale had been blowing hard for three days before a lull in the weather became the first chance my mother had to get some exercise outdoors. She took a stroll to the bottom of the garden, close to her favourite walk along the shores where she had so lovingly and proudly raised her two sons and introduced us to our wonderful lives. Later that day, her body was found there. We all returned to gather at Derrynane once again, this time in mourning.

And so she lies there at rest, close by the abbey ruins near the beach and the harbour overlooked by Bealtra and Bunavalla, with the chorus of the waves and wind in the long dune grass.

And at home.

6

La Vie en France

Netley, England

The ancient cutlass hung in silence on the wall, lit only by weak shafts of streetlight through gaps in the curtain. Nearby, an axe rested alongside a mace and a variety of swords. Well worn through years of use in settling battles and disputes, their presence served as a reminder of times past.

In the distance, the low hum of a large container ship passing along Southampton Water mixed with the light breeze and lapping waves on the shore close to Netley Abbey and on to the entrance of the Hamble River. Otherwise, the house was quiet.

On first introduction, a stranger could easily mistake Paul Standbridge for a latter-day pirate of sorts: tanned and with a gold earring, a piercing stare to match straight-talking wit – almost a real-life version of the fictitious Captain Jack Sparrow of *Pirates of the Caribbean* fame.

The collection of old weapons and first impressions

aside, in fact Standbridge hailed from a respectable English family with no connections to piracy, though a berth in the 1985 Whitbread Round-the-World Race on *Atlantic Privateer* might well be described as swashbuckling; stories of Padda Kuttel's crew racing on the high seas are deeply embedded in sailing lore. And instead of pirates' booty of old, Standbridge's prize was delivering the results to his owner, or at the very least delivering an exceptional experience at the front end of an all-encompassing sport.

It was very early in the morning – too early – and Standbridge was distinctly unimpressed that he was not sound asleep. Restless from lack of sleep caused by concern for a shortlist of unpaid bills that were due, he knew he had to make a decision. As project manager for a private owner he was on the front line. The issue was simple and the solution obvious: the owner would have to be confronted. Lifting the phone, he dialled the errant account.

'Hello? It's Paul here,' he said, the moment the phone answered.

'Eh . . . hello, Paul. What time is it?' The voice was more than a little surprised at the call, enough to be concerned without getting annoyed.

'Four in the morning, but that's not important,' he continued, getting straight to the point. 'Please take out a pen and write down the following names of people you owe money to,' he said. 'When your bank opens tomorrow morning, you're going to go down there and arrange for same-day funds transfers to their accounts.' The message was given, the call ended and by lunchtime the funds were transferred and all was well again.

Straight talking but always polite, a no-nonsense delivery of undertakings and no suffering of fools made for a professional hallmark that immediately instilled confidence amongst fellow sailors, boat owners and team mangers that the job would get done better for Standbridge taking responsibility for it.

And, in any crew position under Standbridge as skipper, whether as a rookie or seasoned campaigner, your standing at a given time could never be in doubt: you either measured up or you didn't. A straight question would reliably receive a straight answer and, in the winter of 1994, sailing as a bowman for Standbridge on a privately owned mid-sized racing boat, the attraction of arriving for a regatta, stepping on board and competing flat out for a week of racing before jumping on a plane again was starting to become too familiar – another challenge was needed.

Not for the first time on the topic, I cornered Standbridge in the middle of a quiet 'after-work' drink at a regatta. I usually managed not to annoy him with trivialities but there were two topics that cropped up from time to time which tested his patience. The first was food, or the lack of it (or at least in the quantities that a hungry twenty-something demanded). His standard reply was typically direct. 'Look, I'm fucking sick of you complaining about being hungry so just fuck off and get a sandwich,' he'd say, adding a cheerful wink for good measure.

The other issue was less straightforward but the solution was quite clear. The great transatlantic races from France that used to arrive into St Barths and the other islands were tremendous battles, lasting for weeks and involving huge preparation and seamanship skills as well as a host of specialities such as weather routing, navigation and tactics. These were not fully crewed boats; sometimes single-handed or at least double-handed, a crew had to be able to perform every role on board.

'If you want more hands-on, why don't you just go and do a Figaro single-handed campaign?' he suggested. 'It's got everything you want – great sailing, campaign management, physically demanding and a really well-organised circuit.' It was also the birthplace of many of the world's best ocean sailors but, being almost exclusively French, presented a host of additional challenges. It also needed money, the kind and amount that was rare at the best of times. Nevertheless, Standbridge was right, it somehow had to be done.

◄○►

In some respects, Standbridge and his experience of more than thirty-five years as a yacht racing professional is unique. Having cut his teeth on private yachts in well-established venues around the Mediterranean, Caribbean and the United States, his time on board *Atlantic Privateer* marked the start of the changeover from the Corinthian owner-driven campaigns motivated as much by competitive drive as spirit of adventure and the make-up of their crews reflected this.

Straddling the 'golden era' of mass participation in sailing that followed in the decades after the Second World War, sailors were soon faced with increasing demands brought on by new technologies such as exotic building materials and innovations such as personal computers and satellite navigation. These permitted almost exponential improvements in performance that could only be met by technically aware, professionally minded sailors who would be best able to commit the time needed to distil these gains for better and better rewards.

The emphasis has now switched from highly effective individual leaders relying on a crew that functions efficiently to a highly effective team relying on efficient individuals within it. The days of owner-driven campaigns dwindled and the unique system that was a curious mix of friendship and fealty between owner and crew became relegated in the face of increasingly structured and managed teams, both afloat and ashore. In the same way as new technology meant boats became lighter, fewer guests were carried on board during racing and even owners themselves could miss out, opting to watch from a spectator boat rather than compromise their team's performance if not up to scratch themselves. Similarly, in place of extended team parties after racing, fitness and dietary regimes became the norm, with socialising often limited to polite cocktail receptions with early finishing times or low-key crew dinners.

The change of gear served to emphasise the difference between the traditional amateur roots of the sport and the professional future that inevitably led to a 'trickle-down' effect as professionals were hired to sail with the keenest owners at the numerous major club and class regattas (which would usually have been amateur events but which also permitted mixed crews).

But the apparent demise of the golden era also led to another major shift. For decades, skippers became household names, even in non-sailing circles, for the achievements delivered in the early days of major races such as the Whitbread Round-the-World Race. Legendary figures such Peter Blake, Grant Dalton, Lawrie Smith and Pierre Fehlmann led crews of more than twenty sailors around the world, not just at sea but taking ownership of their projects, raising the funds personally and becoming expert at almost every aspect of their campaign. With huge personalities to match their ambitions, they became the public face of their projects while their 'production team' – the crew – was delegated to carry out the work. The changing times would lead to workloads more than any one person could reasonably manage in a big-boat team and the skipper's role evolved to become one of facilitator rather than 'all-rounder', someone to coordinate different teams of highly qualified experts within a boat's confined environment. In addition, for higher performances and results, credit would be a shared bounty rather than the exclusive dividend of just one individual.

For Standbridge, the timing was right; he was neatly poised to take advantage of tens of thousands of sea miles on board everything from stripped-down racing boats to high-end superyachts and yet he was still able to change over to the new style of management. Within years of his time on *Privateer*, he too was skippering ocean racers and running inshore day-race crews but not as the head of a rigid command structure, rather as the lynchpin around which an entire crew centred their operations.

His experience was all encompassing and included the America's Cup, Whitbread and Volvo Ocean races and a

146

round-the-world Jules Verne record on *ENZA*, but most importantly he had started out as a top class bowman. So for me, a nipper recently turned full professional, the basics extended far beyond the sharp end of a racing boat and the preserve of a bowman. The old maxim of age bringing moves aft in a boat, first from bow to mid-ships and eventually the cockpit, held true: time served at each position eventually leads to all-round experience.

However, satisfying my need for new challenges whilst at the same time delivering a fulfilling return meant looking beyond the traditional structures of an Anglocentric yachting world, both in terms of thinking and fresh opportunities. Chasing Standbridge's recommendation of pursuing the famous Solitaire du Figaro would inevitably mean one step backwards to take two forward. It would require a return to basics in every aspect, both practical and analytical, to get to grips with a smaller boat plus the rigours of single-handed sailing. It would need support and not just the financial kind but also the benefit of familiar surroundings to shorten the work list of starting a completely new campaign.

It would need a return to the familiar and comfortable, a reliable base camp to take on the task of starting from scratch with responsibilities, not just for crewing a boat, but for doing just about everything from sponsorship and bookkeeping to rigging, boatbuilding and sailing. It was time to return to Ireland and Derrynane. And best of all, it was summer.

―◇―

I returned to Ireland with Standbridge's sharp advice fresh in my mind and fully resolved to act on it or forget it completely. But it was a clear decision and it seemed that it gained momentum immediately. To have backed off, when so many people have helped you attain your goal, would be hard. It was almost a case of 'be careful what you wish for', but I had no regrets at all, despite not having the first clue how exactly the project would pan out.

As with many things in sailing, sooner or later we end up dealing with brass tacks and the inevitability of money, or rather the lack of it. It is an equipment-based sport and while the patronage of an owner who can take care of the financial concerns is an option worldwide for professionals and amateurs alike, it is not a commonplace solution for solo or short-handed sailing.

On return to Derrynane, the slow process of tailoring sponsorship proposal documents to do a 'shotgun' mail-out to every Irish company that might have an interest in a market exposure through a French sailing event got under way. In post-recession Ireland of the mid-1990s it was like sending CVs in search of a job: the occasional 'no thanks' was almost a joy compared to the deafening silence of many. Eventually we were successful when DHL Worldwide Express Couriers replied and a massive hurdle was cleared. I travelled to Dublin, nervously reflecting on the best approach to present my project, poorly aided by my limited knowledge of marketing and sponsorship. 'I mustn't drop the ball now,' I repeated to myself: the door was being opened for me. I was met by Noel Byrne, the Ireland Divisional Manager, who was both friendly and personable.

He explained that DHL Worldwide Express was already sponsoring the Irish driver on the Formula 3 motor circuit, and motor sports were his thing. He admitted to knowing very little about sailing and less about the professional end but he was nevertheless interested. In the unfamiliar environment of a corporate boardroom I laid down the outlines of the campaign, and my passion and enthusiasm must have sold it, because two hours later I was a fully sponsored Irish sailor.

◄○►

I was pretty sure that if I stayed in Ireland and plugged away, eventually a Figaro campaign could lead to a Vendée Globe race entry. But I was also fairly sure it would not be at the level I wanted or on the terms that I would have expected. The centre of activity was France, where the expertise and support of fellow competitors would lift my game; that was the place to be.

With DHL's sponsorship in place, a suitable second-hand boat was located in St Brieux in December 1995. I had worked for a year for Ed Danby who was the skipper of the maxi catamaran *ENZA*. So, after two transatlantics and a period in San Diego during the America's Cup together, he readily agreed to join me for the quick sail to Hamble on the south coast of England for a complete refit and paint job in the sponsor's colours. Two months later, there was another delivery, this time to Kinsale as my adoptive home yacht club to comply with Figaro race rules and finally I was sailing in Irish waters with my own boat. Ahead lay a very challenging few months between training, boat preparations and logistics plus a trip northwards to Ireland's east coast and Howth Yacht Club for sponsorship work with DHL.

France 1997

Inevitably, the move from Ireland to France came around and opportunities began to unfold. A French mate, Sidney Gavignet, introduced me to Michel Desjoyeaux, the country's foremost rising star of the solo ocean-racing scene and in a typically sportsmanlike gesture, he procured an invitation for me to train at the government-funded coaching centre at Port-la-Fôret in Brittany for one year. This was a massive break. Not only was it the first invitation for a non-national but, for a very modest annual licence of around thirty quid, everything at the centre was provided free.

Christian Le Pape managed the Port-la-Fôret Pôle Finistère Course au Large that was a long-established centre of excellence for offshore sailing. All the Figaro sailors started out there and it also developed into support for the Open 60 and trimaran crews. Quite often, the same skippers progressed the whole way through. If there was anywhere in the world to be, this was the place. The small village was a dynamic hub of activity; weekends arrived with the peal of the bell from the Gothic church and a busy market in the village square, mixed with the movement of boats and crews around the marina and boatyards. The surrounding coastline is a maze of rocks, islands and harbours, with the infamous Glenan islands and home to the original outward-bound sailing school just 10 miles offshore. Little did I realise, it would eventually became my home for more than twelve years. The programme included subjects as diverse as how to manage sponsorship, funding, sail design, autopilots, boat branding, electronics and a sound introduction to small-project management. All aspects of training, including physical, mental and dietary, would be covered and we were even to be coached on the water.

By now, the campaign was on a roll and Robert was persuaded to join me from Kerry and agreed to sign on as shore manager. A new camper van would become home, workshop, sail loft and stores as our permanently mobile base for two years. With a clear plan in place, Patrick joined the boat for the delivery trip most of the way to France while Robert started to set up at our first port of call. It was early spring 1997 and, at that time, the Figaro circuit had extensive activities in addition to the single-handed classic race for which it is best known. Early in the season, a week-long speed-trial series was scheduled at the port of Saint-Gilles. The objective was to select an optimum time to set a time for a course out around Îles d'Yeu and back, with the best results of the week taking a share in a prize purse.

As I was arriving around the headland into Saint-Gilles on a calm day with just a light breeze, the great 'Mich Des' was out training to bear witness as my bowman training came good with a slick manoeuvre, which involved gybing the boat whilst simultaneously peeling off one spinnaker to change to another. Impressed, Desjoueaux was very complimentary when we were introduced for the first time in person later that evening. Buoyed by the praise, I began preparations for the time trial on a high.

Within a few days, the wind was up and blowing when my appointed time came around – just minutes before Desjoyeaux's start. Unlike the arrival day, the wind was now more than 25 knots and a crowd had gathered along the shore to watch the trials in the choppy sea state, knowing full well how especially difficult the boats would be to handle in these conditions. Thinking I had the boat set up with water ballast in place and a reef taken in the mainsail, the start should have gone smoothly. But inexperience was about to show and the boat was actually very unbalanced and quickly slammed into a crash-gybe where the mainsail crosses the boat violently before being pinned into the sea on the opposite side.

After a brief battle to restore direction and sail trim, the grim outcome was immediately apparent as the spinnaker had become wrapped around the forestay. Hauling at the foot of the sail failed to bring it back to the deck and I would later learn that the correct solution was to release the halyards holding the sail up and take the 'tuff luff' fitting off the forestay, which would in turn bring the sail down gradually.

Instead, the crewed-boat instinct called for the bowman to rush forward and go aloft. Except there were no others on board to help so a makeshift solution was needed. Pulling the mainsheet in helped heel the boat, placing the mast at an angle so I could free-climb the mast to the top of the forestay. With a death-grip on the rig as it pitched around, I made it to the top and then slid slowly down the forestay, pushing the wrapped spinnaker downwards and eventually gathering it together to reset and work towards making up ground in the wake of Desjoyeaux who had long since started and was blasting ahead without any problems.

It wasn't the prettiest incident and my acrobatics did little to dispel notions of the crazy Irishman amongst the crowds of onlookers on the shore. And if first impressions were to count amongst the established pros, I surely wasn't going to be rated convincingly in the short term.

At least the decent wind allowed me to set a fairly fast time around the course and a smaller runner-up share of the purse took some of the sting of embarrassment away, though what little reputation I had starting the circuit was completely shot after just one week. Clearly, there was a much work to be done and as much learning as only time on the water would allow.

—◦—

The generosity of the French government's sports assistance programme did not quite extend to transforming our language skills overnight but immersion in our campaign soon started overcoming the initial barriers. The Irish and Breton people have a great affinity and the kindnesses we received were many as Robert and I embarked on a full-time campaign. For good measure, we added a special logo to the cockpit of the boat: *Pour être le meilleur, il faut battre les meilleurs* – 'to be the best, you must beat the best'. It was our reminder that we weren't here to mess around and we were not going to let a small thing like a language barrier get in the way.

He drove, I sailed. All over France, from Le Havre to Nantes and on to Spain – Barcelona and Valencia – and then back to Nice before driving up to Belgium; almost everywhere, the build-up to the Figaro race itself with its four offshore stages was supported by a series of local Grand Prix coastal events, a round-Brittany competition plus a Mediterranean circuit. It was hugely challenging round-the-buoy racing and doing everything you do on board a fully crewed boat except doing it all alone and it was some of the best racing ever. For good measure, that winter featured the AG2R transatlantic race.

We became very aware of the responsibilities that a campaign entails and as my boat handling improved rapidly, so too did the simple but essential logistic and planning skills that underpinned a credible entry, which would eventually build a reputation for competence. Winning seemed a long way off, but it was our sole focus and we avoided getting involved in the ex-pat scene or hanging around Irish bars. In fact, there was very little social scene as the end of each day left us too tired for anything but sleep.

In many respects, the Figaro circuit was very similar to the Olympic dinghy circuit but without the constant supervision of national governing bodies with guidelines, selection criteria and very little independence. In the Figaro, one becomes master of one's own destiny and though we did not appreciate it at the time, beholden only to sponsor and self. Before long, all the preparations and training would be put to the test as the main event loomed closer and the summer progressed towards the regular August start.

La Solitare du Figaro 1997

The day arrived and the fleet of fifty boats was watched by a crowd of around 5,000 spectators, lining the shore at

Arcachon, just like the first day in Saint-Gilles three months earlier. In the build-up to the start of the Figaro, our sailmaker had persuaded us that, in spite of my reservations, glued seams rather than the more usual stitched sails would be preferable because they would save weight. But in the minutes before the starting gun fired, in the stress of the countdown in the big fleet, I managed to catch the headsail in a fitting on the spinnaker pole mounted on the deck, and a panel in the sail tore, threatening to rip the sail apart.

As the gun fired and the fleet charged across the line towards Gijon, I found myself climbing the mast once again, this time almost to halfway. I swung out with one hand hanging on, and the other with sticking tape plastering over the tears in the sail to stop it falling apart completely. With the repair complete and holding for the time being, the task of steadily working back up the fleet began.

By now the art of racing a boat single-handed had become a bit easier but I still had a long way to go. For a period, I had been taking catnaps on deck, nervously leaving my semi-reliable autopilot to keep the boat tracking in roughly the right direction. But an incident saw me waking up, standing on the edge of the boat with a light grip on the lifelines as I peered into the night, completely certain I had just seen some phantom passing ship. As I got tired my mind played tricks on me, the instruments became cat's eyes and more phantom ships appeared. In the end I decided it was safer to sleep inside the boat, even for the short ten-minute naps, as the last thing I wanted was to wake up *in* the water. Paranoia was a useful tool to be applied carefully and I would never allow myself to go to sleep if the boat was on a tack that pointed at the shore, even if it was hours away.

Thanks in part to a quick boat, better breeze clear of the main fleet and probably a little luck, I managed to claw back into the front half of the race by the finish of Leg 1. Meanwhile, Juan Merediz won the rookie section of the race into his home waters of northern Spain. However, in preparing the boat for long offshore legs, we had not fitted a decent seat on deck for long periods at the helm and, ashore, Rob was kept busy adapting a boogie board to avoid permanent back problems. On the next leg to Brest, there were no problems and a top third result in the main fleet followed with a strong position for the overall standings amongst the rookies. The third leg was special as it was the traditional stage to Ireland, one rarely missed in the history of the event. The course was around the Fastnet Rock off the west Cork coast, temptingly close to Derrynane, and after having been away for four months, the sight of the familiar coast was like a shot in the arm. After a rounding of the infamous light, we headed eastwards to Kinsale, the colourful fishing town and my adoptive 'home' club. The river estuary protected by Charles Fort marked the welcome finish line as Robert and Sarah, his girlfriend who had been with us all year, jumped on board and we docked to the sounds of congratulations and praise for the first rookie to finish. We were on a high, Robert as much as me, and there was no doubting the positive effect of the homecoming.

But in the overall standings in our division, a thirty-minute lead over Jérémie Beyou in the final leg back to France via the Eddystone Rock lighthouse was to be a nail-biting affair as we fought for the lead against light winds that died completely in the evenings when the sun set. It was a typical night-time 'shut-down' but Beyou had read the conditions better and positioned himself inshore to pick up a marginally better airflow from the evening conditions.

He got across the line first but our thirty-minute lead from the win into Kinsale proved just enough of a buffer for us to take the overall rookie prize and a solid 15th place in the main fleet. We had each won a leg into our home countries: Juan into Spain, myself into Ireland and Jérémie into France. It was a pleasing bonus to be the first non-French winner of the prize as well as the overall rookie winner. However, the Skipper Elf award of a new boat plus budget for the following year was an even bigger boost and payback for the many supporters who had placed faith in our campaign.

Figaro 1998

With sponsorship effectively in place for the following year, we did not have to spend the entire winter hunting for funding and more Figaro class events beckoned including the demanding Transat AG2R from Lorient to St Barths and into the familiar waters of the Caribbean. Sidney Gavignet and I paired up for this two-handed event in March 1998 and after leading the early part of the stage to Madeira where we had a top place finish, we were well placed for the main leg to the Caribbean but in an incredibly tightly packed fleet – the first six boats were one hour apart after a month at sea and 2,600 miles of racing.

The final week became a drag race, and on the last morning of the crossing we rounded the headland of the beautiful French island and it felt like a homecoming. In the bay, we found five other boats simultaneously creeping their way into Gustavia's harbour and though we kept one behind us, we had to be content with fifth place, although we were ahead of several major household names from the French ocean scene. We were satisfied with the knowledge of a job well done. (On the contrary, it is also possible to win a race and still feel like crap because you knew you could have sailed a better race.) Ultimately, the essence of performance for any sportsperson is the pursuit of perfection, winning is only the end result and that is never guaranteed.

Bruno Magras, the harbourmaster, welcomed us 'home' and, with Rob who had flown in to help us ship the boat back to France, we headed through the crowds to my standard landfall – Le Select bar. Sitting under the tamarind trees, we ate our 'cheeseburger in paradise' as it was the same bar that Jimmy Buffet had immortalised in his hit song. Except I had *two* double cheeseburgers with extra fries. I found myself thinking back over the years to the daily catamaran trips to St Barths, being here to watch the multihull ocean races finishing and my earlier dreams of single-handed ocean racing.

With my friends from the island we got the locals' tour of St Barths – table football in the rum shack and Carib beers and chicken wings from the oil-drum barbeques after swimming in the turquoise water. In the evenings we exchanged glasses of Paddy from the bottles Rob had brought with him for '*P'tit punch*' and I was able to share with Rob a big part of my life during those six years when we had not seen each other.

Of significance, perhaps, during that transatlantic with Gavignet, a moment passed when I switched to thinking completely in French as an automatic instinct. Complete immersion over the previous twelve months had removed the language obstacle, admittedly with considerable distance still to travel by way of grammatical correctness.

Once back in France, however, Skipper Elf changed their sponsorship strategy after one of the biggest fraud inquiries since the Second World War led to a review of their marketing campaigns. But for us, though the 1997 Rookie prize was honoured, a sponsorship vacancy now existed. As it happened, a break in the schedule meant taking up an offer to crew for owner Tony Mullins on his *Barlo Plastics* entry for Cork Week in Ireland that summer in a team led by Harold Cudmore and Gordon Maguire. Instead of payment, Mullins agreed to consider a sponsorship proposal for the Figaro that would come to Howth for the second time. With a strong result from my rookie year, the pressure was on to build on that performance; with a fifteenth overall place secured, a podium result was a reasonable target and soon it was Barlo Plastics branding across the hull.

La Solitaire du Figaro 1998

The first leg of the race was from Cherbourg to Howth and, like the previous year, involved grief at the start. It was caused this time by setting off too early and which meant lost time with the obliged sail back along the course to restart after the fleet made its getaway. Also like the previous time, it was a case of slowly working back up through the fleet and by the second night at sea our leading group of boats had reached the Tuskar Rock off the coast of County Wexford. Becalmed and with a foul tide, we all anchored to wait for the north-flowing flood tide and took an opportunity to grab some sleep.

It was a nice idea but we each needed half an eye open for a change in conditions. When the breeze filled in early in the morning, three of us spotted it and weighed anchor while a fourth, who had set his alarm for the change of tide, managed to sleep through both the change of tide and the new wind which promptly died again so he had to stay at anchor for another six hours as we sailed north to Howth. The leading bunch sailed along the banks off the coast of Arklow towards Dublin Bay and while the others who went offshore gained initially, going inside the banks meant tucking in close to the coast as the breeze died in the evening and just making the finishing line before the calm set in completely. I got a full night's sleep in a warm dry bed ashore and the sight of the fleet scattered offshore, still at anchor the next morning, was a good omen for the event, which was decided on accumulated time.

After an inshore course off Ireland's Eye at this first-time Figaro port, we were off again and over the next leg I managed to work *Barlo Plastics* into a strong top ten placing and realistically in the running for the overall win. It was all down to the remaining two legs. Light airs continued to dog the race that year but I was working closely with Steve Hayles, now an experienced navigator and weather expert, to analyse patterns and strategy prior to each stage. It was paying off and shortly after starting the third leg off the Quiberon peninsula, I began to head offshore to get in position for a high-pressure ridge that promised a little extra wind. Suddenly, other boats nearby started gaining ground and then overtaking and opening ground. Something was clearly wrong and a quick inspection revealed a half-sunken fish trap caught around my rudder. It was just out of reach but a little extra stretch would get it. Somewhere in my head was a plan, hatched with very little thought against the sight of the other boats heading away to the horizon, that if I could just reach the trap I could flick it around the rudder and be free again.

Catching the trap but losing balance, I suddenly went overboard and was dragging astern. Clawing frantically hand over hand along the fish trap's thin line only succeeded in pulling me further and further away from my boat and I soon realised I wasn't going to make it back.

Minutes later, Thomas Coville, another competitor on a similar course, spotted my predicament and sailed up alongside me so I could haul myself on board his boat. As my own boat was slowed by the fish trap, we quickly caught up and I stepped across. I managed to thank Thomas as he sailed off, then slumped in the cockpit as I raged with tears of frustration at myself and vented my anger: I had been obliged to accept outside assistance – it was my only option. A similar incident had happened a few years earlier when, during the leg from Ireland to France, race favourite Alain Gautier had been clearing seaweed from his rudder and had fallen overboard. Except this was in deep water north of the

Scilly Islands. As his boat had sailed away, he was left totally alone until, by complete chance, a competitor with a coinciding route spotted what he thought at first to be seagulls until he realised it was a sailor and managed to recover Gautier.

For me, the contest continued and I notified the race committee of the incident and my official retirement from that leg, but I was fuming. I kept going, sailing hard and was rewarded with an unofficial podium position in Gijon. The final stop in northern Spain before the last leg served to get things in perspective again. A lot of hard work from Rob including a good kick in the ass hardened my resolve. Determined not to give up on a good overall place for the entire series, I started the final leg determined to make the most of Hayle's routing advice. His guidance proved sound and I won the leg at the finish in Concarneau with a substantial lead over the fleet of fifty-plus boats. The euphoria of pulling off this significant result eventually wore off and, for a time, it became a bittersweet achievement as I had lost my chance at an overall win due to the man-overboard incident.

Three years of full-time Figaro sailing had delivered some considerable achievements: first non-French winner of the rookie division plus the first non-French overall winner of a stage in the Figaro, and most importantly a much more profound knowledge of what it takes to race and win. But I wondered how something so routine as snagging a fish trap could have cost the campaign whatever the final result would have been. After all, there are so many options available: use a boathook, get a knife and cut the line, maybe back the sails and reverse off the trap. But to reach, no, stretch overboard and risk falling in without using a safety line or anything to secure to the boat was beyond belief. For that crucial split second, I had lost perspective on the situation and I needed to know why.

In those years and occasionally – but thankfully not very often now, I have tended to operate too long in the 'red zone'. The typical manifestation for this is to become very tunnel-visioned and focused exclusively on the problem at hand. But it limits your capacity for delivering the best solution to a problem. It boils down to how much stress you put yourself under in any one job. In routine functions, such as reading, the body is almost at rest with a low heart rate. At the opposite extreme, intense physical activity raises the heart rate beyond maximum levels that reduce capacity for coordinated, logical thought. Sailing, and especially single-handed sailing, simply cannot allow operating in the 'red zone'. It was clearly vital to be aware of the risk and to learn when to say 'enough' and find a solution that worked. To maintain optimum performance physically and mentally means not being overstressed. Emotions had to be controlled and used sparingly. Another lesson learnt.

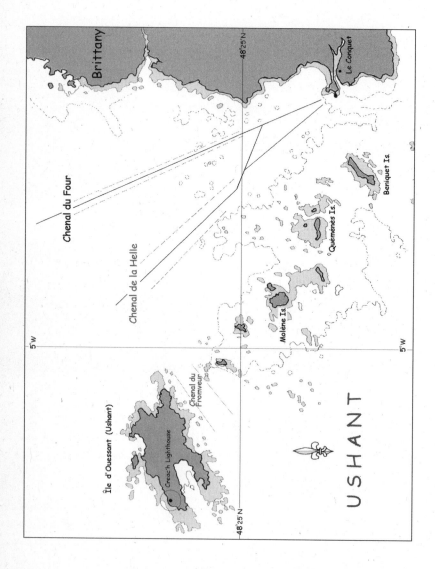

Brittany

Chenal du Four

Chenal de la Helle

Le Conquet

48°25'N

Beniquet Is.

Quéménès Is.

Molène Is.

5 w

5 w

Île d'Ouessant (Ushant)

Creac'h Lighthouse

Chenal du Fromveur

48°25'N

USHANT

7

Racing the World

Newport, Rhode Island

The gale blew hard outside but the sound lulled me to sleep quickly. The soft pillow and warm quilt were a welcome change to a damp sleeping bag and a narrow bunk at sea; the sound of the tall pine trees surrounding Newport's historic Jailhouse Inn were a contrast to the creaking of winches and deck gear.

In the depths of my slumber, I could hear a strange noise and voice began calling to me.

Tap-tap.

'Damian!'

Tap-tap-tap.

'Damian, help me!'

The voice persisted, echoing around my dreams, insisting on my attention. Gradually, a ghostly vision joined in, fading in and out, strangely real and looking remarkably like Liam, our team boatbuilder, who had been with us at dinner earlier. It had been an upbeat evening, almost a celebration at the end of a long period of boat preparation and plenty of hard work as we prepared *Playstation* for a transatlantic record attempt. Our navigator Stan Honey had arrived and everyone except our skipper/owner Steve Fossett was there: we were ready to go. Hard-working, hard-playing Liam had left us to meet friends from Rhode Island. We were sharing a room but there was no sign of him before I hit the sack. The vision appeared again and this time I was definitely awake; it was real and it was 3.00 a.m.

Tap-tap.

The face appeared fleetingly at the rain-lashed window. In an instant, it appeared again as Liam himself swung out of the tip of a small pine tree, barely able to swing back in a few feet to tap the window of our second-floor room before the breeze caught him again. With a sheepish grin, he lost his grip and slid down the branches to land heavily in the garden below. I ran downstairs and unlocked the front door as he stumbled in, covered in pine leaves and mud, mumbling something about the night porter and what a great night he'd had. The next morning, as we arrived at the boat straight from the gym, Liam was already hard at work and seemingly no worse for wear, despite his late-night adventures.

After working up the boat to full readiness, we swapped one historic hotel for another as we sailed south to New York. There the Chelsea Hotel would be our home on standby for the start of the crossing while the boat was docked nearby in the shadow of the twin towers of the World Trade Centre. We stayed there for its convenience to the dock at Battery Park and Pier 54 where the *Titanic* should have arrived. Superstars from the artistic, literary and entertainment worlds have made the low-key hotel famous as their home for extended periods: Bob Dylan, Janis Joplin, Leonard Cohen, Iggy Pop, Stanley Kubrick, Dennis Hopper, Eddie Izzard, Uma Thurman, Elliot Gould, Jane Fonda, Henri Cartier-Bresson, Brendan Behan, The Grateful Dead, Madonna, Jimi Hendrix and Sid Vicious, to name but a very few. Against this backdrop, I met Steve Fossett, world-famous adventurer and a millionaire celebrity in his own right.

–◆〇◆–

Fossett was an extraordinary character: focused, driven and yet introverted. He took goal-setting to a whole new level and his accomplishments inspired all those who encountered him. From a fortune he made as an options trader, the former Merrill Lynch commodities-salesman-turned-entrepreneur had become independently wealthy and could finance his ambitions. But these were not simple dreams.

Best known as an aviator, he relentlessly pursued extreme adventures in balloons, gliders, and powered aircraft as well as in sailing, a cousin of flight from shared aerodynamic theory. He was also a climber of mountains, large and small, and could not easily resist even a hill climb when visiting new places. In his adventure career, he reportedly set ninety-one aviation world records, twenty-six sailing world records and climbed the highest peaks on six continents.

Things did not always go according to plan, though. He swam the English Channel after four attempts, in the process recording one of the slowest times ever. He took two attempts to complete the extreme Iditarod Dog-Sled Race in Alaska, from Anchorage to Nome over 1,050 miles. The dogs needed a real team leader whom they knew and respected; Fossett was to learn on his first attempt that there were no shortcuts to preparing for this race – time was needed – a lesson that was to stand him in good stead later on.

It was not simply that he was an aviator or a sailor or a mountaineer or a scout, he was a record-breaker constantly in search of delivering more than just personal bests. By the time his adventure career was at its peak, he had set in motion handfuls of projects, managed by experts on his behalf until the critical stages when he could arrive and take over. He had previously owned *Lakota*, a trimaran on which he set a dozen records both single-handed and crewed, many of which stand unbroken, such as the Round Ireland record in 1993 with a time of 44 hours and 42 minutes – that's an average speed of 16 knots.

In the case of *Playstation*, his core team comprised the boat's designer, Gino Morelli, plus his watch captains Ben Wright and Brian Thompson, the latter of whom I met in San Diego in 1999. Fossett had been persuaded to enter The Race, a non-stop, no-size-limits, round-the-world sailing race with a US$2 million prize organised by French sailor Bruno Peyron who, in turn, was the first winner of the Jules Verne Trophy in 1993 for completing a round-the-world record time of less than eighty days.

The line-up of seven boats was comprised of not just a selection of the best ocean-going crews in the world but the boats themselves earned the fleet of super-maxi catamarans its own designation of 'G-class' or Giant class. The smallest boat was 86 feet long but the leading contenders were well over 100 feet and were led by Grant Dalton's *Club Med*, Loick Peyron's *Innovation Explorer* and Cam Lewis' *Team Adventure*.

But we had a record attempt to consider first. Although Fossett had now joined his team, Wright as team director led the briefings ashore, while on board Thompson took the lead. But the owner was hardly a passenger and as skipper was involved with many of the critical decisions. He consulted closely with Stan Honey, arguably the best ocean navigator in the world, and the pair would spend hours below checking weather updates that would inform both the decision to begin the record attempt and our routing once under way.

Transatlantic Record Attempt: Ambrose Light, NY, to The Lizard, UK

We had a glamour run after leaving the Big Apple and passing the famous Ambrose Lighthouse with perfect timing behind an eastbound high-pressure system that left flat seas behind and just ahead of a mounting depression that could be relied upon for steady winds. Fossett took his turn at the helm and the big cat powered away from the coast, the leeward bow sending spray metres into the air and swirling away behind us. A mile was ticked off every couple of minutes as the hours of each watch went by and we were on record pace. We blasted out past Martha's Vineyard, Boston, Nova Scotia and on towards Sable Island.

Famed for its 350 recorded shipwrecks, treacherous currents, thick fog and hundreds of feral horses left to live on what barely amounts to a 20-mile sandbar on the western edge of the Atlantic, Sable Island has left a significant mark on maritime history. On 30 July 1894 the New Brunswick barque *Nicosia*, on a voyage from Dublin to St Johns, ran aground in thick fog. She was a total loss but all of her crew was saved. By contrast in the summer of 1926 and August 1927, the Lunenburg fishing fleet was caught in ferocious storms leading to the loss of 138 lives. Many came from the same small Nova Scotia fishing villages and their deaths had a devastating effect on their communities.

By Cape Race, we were still looking good for the record but, ahead of the low-pressure system, the seaway was slowly becoming rougher. On the third day, mid-Atlantic, we were still on pace but the low-pressure system had slowed down and we gradually fell behind the existing record time. We spent the frustrating final days of the crossing in a series of gybes that slowed our more direct route and we finished off Cornwall just outside the record.

Southampton, UK

Either way, the transatlantic journey was significant preparation for The Race and highlighted the need for major modifications to the boat so we sailed straight to Lymington on the Solent where we got to work on a major refit led by Liam.

The boat at 105-feet was overpowered by the 147-foot rig so the decision was taken to extend the length by 20 feet, making it the largest entry in The Race. At that time, it was the largest floating structure ever built in carbon. After being hauled out at Green Marine, both bow sections were cut off and new bow sections were constructed, then 'scarfed in' to make the front of the boat much higher as well as longer. It was a big project, which cost Fossett a huge amount of money.

Midway through the refit, Ed Danby called me with an offer of a place with Dalton on *Club Med*. It was a super opportunity – the right skipper, best boat and a great crew – and it would certainly open up other opportunities. I racked my conscience and tried to be objective. For two nights I slept badly, and then realised that was the answer: I had to be comfortable with the decision. I had accepted a place on Fossett's team so could hardly break my word to him; it is hard to let someone down. I was also mindful of what Gordon Maguire had told me about his experience ten years previously when he jumped ship from *NCB Ireland* to the British entry and key rival *Rothmans* in the Whitbread Round-the-World Race. Maguire had been a late selection for the Irish boat, recruited after successfully helming *Jamarella* for *Rothmans* skipper Lawrie Smith in the British Admiral's Cup team of 1989. The Howth sailor was the rising star of offshore sailing and his presence on the *NCB Ireland* crew list was a morale boost. But when the boat failed to perform in the first leg of the race from

Southampton to Uruguay, Smith poached Maguire and fellow crew member Henry Hiddes from South Africa. Far away, back in Ireland, there was uproar.

Maguire said at the time, 'I just thought this was another Irish boat having a go; I didn't realise it was *the* Irish boat that had the whole country following it.' He told me all about it during the 1995 Admiral's Cup, but it was a full decade after the incident before his side of the story was fully accepted at home. However, he went on to become one of the most sought after offshore helmsmen in the world and his move to *Rothmans* was key to that outcome.

In the autumn of 1999, just as we prepared to sail from the Solent on our giant catamaran for the start line of The Race in Barcelona, Fossett announced to us out of the blue that The Race was not really his thing and he wanted to make a Jules Verne Trophy attempt instead. We were all floored. Having missed out on the *Club Med* offer, I was more than unhappy with his decision. The other crew, Mikey Joubert and Nick Maloney, and even Morelli, Wright and Thompson who were the closest to the skipper, were all dumbfounded as we were all hooked by the concept of The Race.

We were in crisis just weeks before the start and a group formed to discuss how to deal with the issue. It seemed quite possible that Fossett had never wanted to do The Race, preferring instead to add to his string of records. But he had not levelled with us earlier that he was unhappy. Although Morelli argued that Fossett was the boss, his heart was not in his defence. This wasn't a mutiny: we were ashore and fully entitled to express ourselves. We weren't going for the jugular, but we needed to object constructively. A meeting was called and a room booked in our hotel.

Fossett sat down and calmly listened to each of us who spoke, setting out the issues and outlining the effort and preparation that had gone into getting *Playstation* ready for The Race. He mentioned his preference for record challenges. Then he sat quietly and when we had finished, he reflected to himself for about two or three minutes. As we waited for his response, I wondered to myself if we had overdone our appeal. After all, he had spent a small fortune refitting the boat and he clearly wanted results, which meant records set on his terms. And then he spoke, calmly and without rancour or even a hint of bitterness.

'Okay guys, we're going to do The Race.'

And that was it. He had decided after listening to us; there would be no reversals and it was full steam ahead. Incredibly, we had got our way; it's not every day that a millionaire changes his mind based on his crew's opinions. So we continued on as planned to Barcelona, home of Gaudí and the Sagrada Família, a city planning to mark the new millennium by staging the ultimate round-the-world race.

The Race, 2000: Barcelona to Barcelona, Round the World Non-stop

On 1 January 2000, as the city celebrated the new millennium, the fleet blasted away from Barcelona and headed south towards the Alboran Sea and approaches to the Strait of Gibraltar. It was quite an emotional departure and tensions were running high. Already, the innovative

Team Philips led by Pete Goss had been forced out when their boat broke up during an ill-fated training session a month earlier that had seen all the crew airlifted off the boat very far north in the Atlantic. Similarly, Peyron's *Team Explorer* had also come close to ending their hopes before the race began in a near-capsize on the delivery to the start. This was uncharted territory, sending unproven and unrestricted boats into the depths of the world's oceans in the full knowledge that everything would be at the limits and that nobody had sailed such boats around the planet before. This was frontier stuff and unseen in popular sailing since the days of Sir Francis Chichester.

The boats were limited in size only by the technology available and principally by structural tolerances. Maximum winch sizes decided the maximum loads the boats could tolerate and in turn placed limits on size. More recently, technological advances have varied the sizes upwards though inevitably, budgets can only accommodate so much and human endurance has its limits also. The Race was the ultimate challenge of its time.

Even before we left the Med, we had serious sail issues: a stop was needed and so we pulled into Gibraltar. A crane was hired and between it and the crew, we manhandled the sails up onto the dock and onto a forklift truck. At the local loft, the sailmaker realised that his sewing machine could not handle the heavy material and after repairing what he could, they were craned onto the boat again and we left twenty-four hours later. Bitterly disappointed that we had lost valuable time for the stop, after sixteen days at sea during which we made a little progress towards catching the fleet, we were 1,000 miles behind when our daggerboard snapped. Although the gap to the fleet was still surmountable by ocean-racing standards, Fossett gathered us together on deck. It was time to call it a day. We could of course carry on and perhaps get lucky but instead, here off Cabo Frio, he pulled the plug and we turned northwards. Needless to say, we agreed this time because we were at sea where there is a clear distinction from ashore where you have an opinion: once afloat, there is no doubt that the final call rests with the skipper.

So we pulled out of The Race and were soon heading away from the fleet, each making 500-plus mile days so that we soon became thousands of miles apart. But we were not the only ones to have problems. Cam Lewis and Randy Smyth on *Team Adventure* set a blistering pace from the outset but were being hunted down by Dalton's more experienced crew on *Club Med*. Then the steering cable jumped off *Club Med*'s port steering quadrant, causing the boat to round up and broach, almost to the point of capsize as it had been blasting along under full mainsail. Neal McDonald was at the helm and, as a newcomer to large multihulls, he had listened carefully to the advice given by veteran Hervé Jan who warned that, in a capsize situation, these boats were so large there would be time to run for the cabin: in deep ocean, staying attached to the boat was a matter of life or death.

'We were belting downwind at 35 knots in pitch darkness with a massive gennaker up when it happened,' McDonald later recalled. 'I thought our rudder had broken as there was no steering.' All on deck froze as the boat heeled towards capsize as it rounded up. I was terrified, and anyone in such situations who says they aren't is either stupid or a liar.'

The crew piled on deck as the giant cat levelled off and began furling the huge sail. McDonald stepped across to the starboard helm which was working and, within twenty minutes, *Club Med* was on its way again. Eventually, only Dalton's boat made it around relatively unscathed despite the nasty broaching incident and he lifted the trophy as the winner. Contrast that to Lewis on *Team Adventure* who had several crew injured in the first half of the course and had to pull into Cape Town to let them off the boat; just finishing the race was a considerable achievement. And *Explorer*, which was plagued with sail problems continuously, also managed to complete the course.

After a 24-hour pit stop in Antigua – we were nearby and it was too tempting to pass by, especially as we were not due back for two months – for food and beers, we sailed on to Charleston in West Virginia. But there was a snag. The plan for The Race had never anticipated stopping for any reason in the United States as it was nowhere near the course track. Which meant many of the crew did not have the required B1/B2 visas to enter the USA. On arrival, we were escorted to the immigration building. Thankfully, my passport carried the stamp. Even better, my immigration officer had Irish ancestry. Already, a poor view had been taken of Fossett for bringing a bunch of illegal aliens into the States. He faced a fine of US$10,000 – per person. We listened to the officers discussing the case; it seemed they were going to use the opportunity to train a junior member in the not-so-subtle art of grilling aliens and it was not going to be a pleasant experience. And as far as my Irish-American officer was concerned, the presence of two British nationals on board was an extra special reason to be particularly rigorous. In the end, Fossett was able to pull a few strings and all was smoothed over or at least without spending US$90,000 in fines.

Although there was another more local event that interested Fossett, I left the boat in Charleston as there was a possibility of a place on a Volvo Ocean Race team coming up. The lure of racing around the world had now firmly grasped me, yet the notion of doing it on the biggest boat possible meant that the G-Class multihull challenge was unfinished business for me as much as for Fossett: for all of us, in fact.

This was only the beginning of a series of circumnavigation projects, either race- or record-based and, like this first attempt, not all would work out according to plan.

The Jules Verne Record, 2002: Non-stop Round-the-World

Finishing with *Playstation* nevertheless opened up a world of opportunities that were the fast track to full involvement at cutting-edge transoceanic races. It was the start of a train of projects that rapidly launched me into living my ultimate dream of racing for a living, being at sea, constantly being challenged and of learning new skills and techniques, whether in preparations ashore or improving performance afloat. Best of all, a long-standing goal of competing for the Whitbread Round-the-World Race (it had become the Volvo Ocean Race in 2001) was a reality. My first full circumnavigation of the planet in this epic race arrived with an opportunity to join the campaign on board *Team Tyco* with Kiwi skipper Kevin Shoebridge. It was a complete start-to-finish effort that encompassed all the essential stages of a prolonged campaign. For me, it was the opportunity to get an insight into the running of a top class professional team.

Ultimately, our fourth place overall in the fleet of eight 60-foot monohulls meant we missed out on the podium but it was against the backdrop of the third generation of this class of boat delivering some incredibly tight finishes. And it was the mastery of American John Kostecki who skippered the overall winner, *Illbruck,* that pointed towards the need for early preparedness; a lesson that would be taught again in the coming edition. The previous 1997–1998 race had not even ended when this German project was announced. The other lesson that would be learned was the need to develop technically as the race progressed and this was delivered by Neal McDonald, who skippered *Assa Abloy* and kept *Illbruck* under constant pressure, especially towards the end of the race to take second overall.

But the lure of racing the world non-stop in maxi multihulls remained strong even after the intensity of a fifteen-month Volvo campaign. Soon after the race finished in Kiel, I was back in France. Ellen MacArthur had also been attracted to the notion of a G-class campaign for the Jules Verne Trophy. She had finished second overall in the Vendée Globe in 2001 and had shot to stardom, both in England and in France where she was dubbed '*La petite Anglaise*'. Her achievement was considerable and even the most die-hard sceptics were silenced or at least acknowledged that she had something exceptional, that her hard work and aptitude were real. We had known each other from our time spent in the Figaro circuit and I used to see her around Hamble Yacht Services, a mecca for sailing on the Solent. She was very enthusiastic and, though not especially experienced early on, she was well received by all who were happy to wait and see what results she would deliver. At that time, she also sailed against Mark Turner, who would become her business partner and as a publicist also handled the PR for my Figaro campaigns. Eventually, the pair started their hugely successful and groundbreaking Offshore Challenge business.

MacArthur has a very natural, open personality that is warm and empathetic. She is more than just a good technical sailor: her management skills, particularly time management, are also very strong. Together with Turner, she has a winning combination. In the aftermath of her success in the Vendée Globe race, she had her eye on the Jules Verne. By then, UK interest in the Whitbread/Volvo race was waning as short-handed sailing as well as the BT Global Challenge – pay-to-play for amateurs – began to capture popular attention. It was also around the time that Francis Joyon took de Kersauson's G-class boat, which he had raced fully crewed and sailed single-handed round the world, a superhuman feat that set him apart as a true giant amongst ocean sailors with a new time for the round-the-world single-handed of 72 days 22 hours. Four years later, he was to take another fifteen days off his own time.

As a handover for the boat, together with Ellen, Neal McDonald and Anthony Merrington, we made an attempt on the Round Britain and Ireland race in 2002 on *Orange*, an older Giles-Ollier-designed 110-footer. Afterwards the boat was refitted to become *Kingfisher B&Q*. We got ready to leave for our start base in Lorient at the old campaign HQ for the French America's Cup team *Le Défi*. Watch captains Hervé Jan, McDonald and Guillermo Altadill ran the programme while Neil 'Albert' Graham managed the shore programme with Johnny Mordaunt as boat captain. Our training that winter was the coldest sailing ever: it was too rough to go offshore, so we hugged the coast doing long windward–leeward legs instead.

Mid-English Channel, Just North of Ushant

In the days leading up to the start, the team moved from 'no-go' to 'standby' and eventually to 'we're off' when the crew would assemble and sail out to the starting area. Hervé Jan and Ronan le Goff lived up the road from me and we had been doing the joint 50-mile car run to Lorient and back each day during the last two months before the start of the record attempt. Both pure Breton, Jan still spoke the language with his parents while Le Goff lived in a beautifully renovated farmhouse next to his folks who looked after it while he was at sea.

The green light was on, given by our navigator who had spotted the ideal window in which to leave. 'Meeting tomorrow morning at 0530 for dock-off at 0630' was the order as we drove home together to pack our sea bags for two months. Except that the idea of a few after work beers was proposed and by 11 p.m. the table in Le Goff's living

Day 3 of the Archipelago Raid 2006 off Nagu, Finland, with Magnus Woxen.
(*Courtesy* Thierry Martinez/Sea&Co)

Magnus 'Baggy' Woxen at the helm with chart book during the Archipelago Raid 2006. (*Courtesy* Thierry Martinez/Sea&Co)

IMOCA Open 60-footer *Paprec Virbac* on a training sail for the
Barcelona World Race. (*Courtesy* Thierry Martinez/Sea&Co)

Race winners J. P. Dick (right) and Damian arriving into the dock at the end of the Barcelona World Race 2008.

(*Courtesy* David Branigan/Oceansport)

County colours and friends from Kerry greet the winners on arrival in Barcelona.
(*Courtesy* David Branigan/Oceansport)

Suzy-Ann and Damian at the welcome party in Barcelona.
(*Courtesy* David Branigan/Oceansport)

Green Dragon at the team base in Cape Town at the end of Leg 1 of the 2008–2009 Volvo Ocean Race. (*Courtesy* David Branigan/Oceansport)

Green Dragon skipper Ian Walker is welcomed to Cochin, India.
(*Courtesy* David Branigan/Oceansport)

Phil 'Wendy' Harmer gets a taste of real food on *Green Dragon*'s arrival in Boston, courtesy of Good Food Ireland's Maurice Keller.

(*Courtesy* David Branigan/Oceansport)

Green Dragon bursts into the lead at the start of Leg 7 in Boston.

(*Courtesy* David Branigan/Oceansport)

Damian and Oisín are reunited after Leg 7 of the Volvo Ocean Race
in Galway, 2009.

(*Courtesy* David Branigan/Oceansport)

room was full of empty bottles and the *craic* was flowing well. I eventually left the lads, who had opened another bottle of Breton cider, and wandered back to the house, which I somehow managed to find.

An hour or two later, the alarm clock rang with brutal intensity and a terrible realisation struck: I still hadn't packed my bags, it was 4.30 a.m. and I had twenty minutes to be on the road. Adrenaline overcame the haze as gear, clothes, torches, knives and various equipment were thrown into two bags.

'Jaysus, don't forget the sea boots,' I mumbled to myself as I cut the electrical breakers, turned off the water at the mains and stumbled out on the road to meet my buddies. (The unlocked door would remain like that for the next two months.) By 5.05 a.m. there was no sign of them. In the cold morning air I got out my phone and rang both numbers: no answer. Maybe they had already gone, forgotten me in their own haze – no, not possible. All the same, in a minor panic I rang the base. No, the lads hadn't shown up and where the hell were we. About another twenty minutes later, the beaten-up Peugeot 405 came into view, both windows down and the two boys with sunglasses on despite the fact that it was still dark. '*Putain les gars* – we're bloody late . . .' And the stench of alcohol almost knocked me out as I squeezed in the back seat. With a smile as my own head started to thump, I put on my sunnies and settled down for the drive to Lorient.

◄○►

We left the dock as the strong westerlies became north-westerly, indicating the ideal weather pattern. Some of the crew was sick as we waited off the coast for the start in freezing air temperatures though, funnily enough, the three party boys were unaffected. As we went to take in a reef, we discovered a problem. Le Goff, still smiling from the night before, was hoisted aloft and confirmed that the mainsail track was damaged. Luckily, Tracy Edwards and Brian Thompson had their own G-class *Maiden* almost readied for their own record attempt but kindly allowed us to take the track from their boat in Southampton.

The start was delayed as we sailed across the channel, hoping the weather window, a two- to three-day period of northwest winds, would remain open. A Jules Verne round-the-world record attempt is a seasonal thing and squeezed by the short Southern Ocean summer. The earliest possible start is October while a departure after the end February leaves you still trying to exit the South Pacific with the first autumn depressions arriving at the Horn. Time was ticking by as we sailed to Falmouth and anchored while Albert rushed from the Solent with the spare part for us.

Back at sea and shortly after the start, we were making 450 miles a day but the seas were pounding us. On the first night, one of our two Fleet 77 satellite domes was blown clean off the deck. The next day, the cover was blown off the second dish. Jason Carrington did an amazing job repairing it but in the process discovered that the salt water had damaged a resistor. So he made up a new one from a piece of carbon and found the correct resistance by stripping away strands of carbon until it was right: the system suddenly powered up and we were back in business. We could stay in touch with shore and receive weather data.

We enjoyed a good run south through the Atlantic, crossing the Doldrums and around the St Helena High. Occasionally, we would receive a visit from a whale or some dolphins but otherwise, aside from the visits of deepwater sea birds and our own company, these were the only hints of life on the planet for weeks and even months on end. And still we went south, until, as a surprise, we passed close to Gough Island off Tristan da Cunha. This is as far you can get from mainland in this part of the world and the island loomed up out of the fog as a reminder that we were now entering a new realm, that of the albatross and the deep Southern Ocean, a place of constant low-pressure systems, huge waves and icebergs. Desolate and abandoned other than a small manned weather station, it was the gateway to the Southern Ocean and further than we had reached with Fossett just three years earlier. We put up a fractional spinnaker with the reefed main and were sailing south, deep and fast, having sighted the island's ancient landing place. Within half an hour, the island returned to the fog in our wake. We surfed hard south for a full week before turning eastwards until the approach to the Kerguelen Islands where the waves were steep, at least 20 feet high, with some breaking impressively.

That night, still under spinnaker, a bad command to coordinate a gybe took Ellen by surprise as she trimmed the traveller sheet. The load on the winch caused the plastics in the rope to melt onto the drum. The jagged edges ran through her hand and sliced open her palm, which needed stitches. She went below to be treated by our navigator/ medic and, within

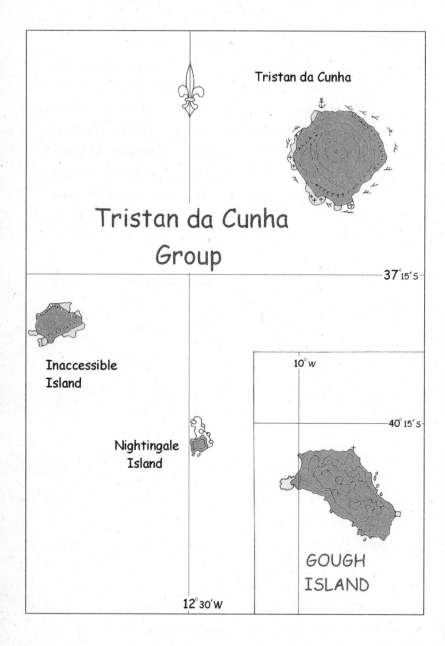

Tristan da Cunha

Tristan da Cunha Group

37°15′S

Inaccessible Island

10°W

40°15′S

Nightingale Island

GOUGH ISLAND

12°30′W

an hour, she was back on deck as if nothing had happened. Unlike other sports, in sailing, men and women can compete alongside one another as equals. In her case, she simply set the right tone, delegated and let people get on with their jobs.

As we left the Kerguelen plateau in our wake, late that night I woke suddenly to feel the giant cat lurch, and braced myself for what I thought was surely a capsize. The boat stayed upright and people were running around on deck and shouting. The rig had fallen down. On deck it was pitch black and organised chaos as the operation to cut the mast away had already started. Our record attempt was over but our options were limited: we were 100 miles east and downwind of the Kerguelens where a group of isolated French scientists lived. Even if we could have sailed back upwind to the islands, there wouldn't have been any solutions there either. The only alternative was to sail 3,000 miles to western Australia.

McDonald set up the massive boom to go upright by using a jury-rigged tripod and we could now fashion sails to drive us. Without the stability of the rig, the platform, released from the tension of the rigging, would have lurched itself apart. Diagonal wires were led across from each hull and tensioned hard to assist. We then spent three weeks sailing to Perth, still managing to reach speeds of 15 knots at times. No longer in competition mode, it was vital for everyone to stay occupied by getting into a rhythm that would last for the duration of the voyage. Someone made up a chessboard from sailcloth and bits of old materials and a league got going, which kept lethargy at bay until we spotted land.

It was to be my second time into Fremantle in similar

circumstances but not my last. We had a swim at Cottesloe Beach, drank beers at the Norfolk Inn and enjoyed a true Aussie town that managed to retain its outback tradition despite being a suburb of Perth. Our on-board cameraman, Andrew 'Jack' Preece, made a beautiful film for the BBC called *In the Eye of the Storm* which was a wonderful way of depicting the project despite the lack of a sporting outcome, ultimately turning what could have been a failure into a successful result for the sponsor.

Plymouth, UK, 2003

Barely four years after our first meeting, I was back with Fossett on board *Playstation*, now renamed *Cheyenne* after the Native American people. The boat had aged considerably but with good reason. Amongst his brace of records, Fossett had retraced his steps in 2001 and set a new transatlantic record time of 4 days 17 hours. However, the following year, Bruno Peyron set a new Jules Verne Trophy record, shattering Olivier de Kersauson's five-year-old time by more than a week. The new target to beat was 64 days, 8 hours, 37 minutes 24 seconds; technology was changing the game, tightening the margins and making the improved record times harder to achieve.

Yet Fossett was unfazed and just as determined. It was typical of his character – unflappable. You simply had to be in awe of his accomplishments and when the call came to join the boat once more, it was for me unfinished business. But even though sailing with him was a career highlight for me, in spite of his wealth the team set-up was not the best funded so there were compromises. Fossett carefully managed his wealth as many of his goals and records required a significant amount of capital outlay – one balloon attempt cost $1.5 million and he was playing at a level completely inaccessible to most people. For this attempt, we would have a crew of thirteen, led by Fossett as usual but managed by Dave Scully, his boat captain who had set twelve previous records with the owner. He would be a watch captain opposite Thompson and Jacques Vincent, with Adrienne Cahalan as navigator.

When we discussed the need for a top bowman, it was easy to introduce Justin Slattery who proved to be a key crew member. We had sailed against each other in the Volvo race when he was on *News Corp* with skipper Jez Fanstone, a campaign that followed a series of progressive crew places for him on maxi boats. He too had been in contact with the *NCB Ireland* campaign when his father brought him down to see the boat on a coastal tour when it stopped off in Dunmore East, County Waterford. From that moment, he was hooked on a career in sailing and did some initial training at Eddie English's International Sailing Centre in Cobh. Multihulls were new to him and, like all of us, he quickly learned how to cross the boat safely via the trampoline, avoiding the full waves as they pass through the netting or the marginally less risky option of running across the centre beams, which is often the preferred technique.

The team gathered around the boat in Falmouth, the ideal base to reach the start/finish line formed by the Créac'h lighthouse on Ouessant (Ushant) Island, France, and the Lizard Lighthouse in England. Not too far away, de

Kersauson was watching the weather with his crew on the trimaran *Geronimo* for an attempt to regain his former record from Peyron. We had the prospect of company.

In the end, however, we opted for an earlier weather window. By its nature, the start of a Jules Verne attempt is a windy affair as you typically leave in the northwest gale that follows the passage of a cold front. But the conditions in the English Channel were the worst I had ever seen, similar to what *ENZA* had encountered on their successful Jules Verne record attempt in 1994. They had finished with warps and chains streamed from the back of the boat to try and slow it down in the huge storm-driven seas. For us, the first few days put enormous stress on the boat as we blasted southwards, immediately running up 500-plus miles per day, which we badly needed to break Peyron's record.

After three weeks at sea, mostly spent in the tropics, we were going well, though the heat of the region was difficult to deal with. The balance between staying dry wearing foul weather gear or accepting to be wet and just wearing shorts is not easy and the choice is personal. The aggravating factor is salt and the lack of freshwater: salt mixed with Gore-Tex gear creates skin chafe, which can easily become infected, so most sailors wear a thin layer of full thermals underneath when they have their foulies on.

Crewman 'Martin' had been wearing his foulie bottoms for the best part of two weeks non-stop when he announced that he had a problem. Not knowing the full extent or the exact area of difficulty, the guys on deck called up the medic.

'Martin seems to have some chafe issues. Can you help?'

However, in the routine patient–medic questioning prior to inspection, it transpired that 'Martin' hadn't been wear *anything* under his foulies.

'I think that I'm going to have to add a new illness into the on-board medic's journal,' said our carer, delivering his diagnosis publicly. 'It's called "Gore-Tex knob" and I'm pretty sure that you are going to die from it.'

By the time we had passed through the South Atlantic, on the approaches to the deadly Southern Ocean, *Cheyenne* had started to protest. Either through a gas leak or just poor planning, we discovered that we had run out of the fuel and we had only just passed south of Cape Town. We wouldn't be able to feed ourselves unless something radical happened. The solution fell to Slattery whose relationship with the dry locker where he stood keeping warm when off-watch was brought to an end. He took the small diesel-powered heater and built an oven in which he was able to boil water in a pressure cooker so we could eat our freeze-dried food. Result!

Our next major shock came when the forestay holding the rig in place started to come apart. The heavy di-formed wire that led into a Norseman cone fitting had pulled out under huge loads. The mast, already raked backwards in its normal setting, was being held up by the headsail and inner forestay but this would not last. The situation looked bad: if the rig failed, it would fall backwards and smash through the aft beam that joined *Cheyenne*'s twin hulls. We would certainly have to abandon ship and, 1,000 miles south of the Cape of Good Hope, this wasn't a pretty prospect, not least because of the near gale conditions we were sailing in or the worse weather to come.

I was hoisted aloft as the pressure was eased off the rig and we began limping towards Cape Town as a safety precaution. But the boat continued to move wildly in the well-built seaway and the motion was magnified close to the top of the 147-foot rig. Looking down, the crew seemed like miniature figures jumping about the trampoline between the hulls as we prepared to strip the forestay and attempt the repair.

The first job was to take down the furling gear, which consisted of long sections of aluminium tubing. Backing off the screws until just a thread held the extrusions in place, we slid the sections down the forestay onto the netting below in a delicate and dangerous process – as demonstrated when one dropped off and shot spear-like through the trampoline and into the ocean.

On inspection, Scully and Slattery found that the Norseman fitting had simply slipped and all the parts were still there. The Norseman cone was the size of a small artillery shell. One belt of it, should it swing loose, could ruin your day – or worse. Scully and Slattery got to work their magic by taking the end of it to the base of the mast, which then became an outdoor workshop. With limited tools, they managed to rethread each strand of thick wire until eventually the terminal fitting could be slipped back into place and the forestay was almost as good as new.

We had not been quite hove to but were making about 5 knots in the heavy seaway. Less than eighteen hours later, the struggle to ease the massive weight forward and back into place on the front beam began. Fighting the swaying of the 100-foot stay meant reducing the sag to get the lower end to join up and there was a final battle involving near misses until suddenly the pin slotted in and there was a roar: 'the forestay is back!'

During that time we sewed hanks onto the headsail so we could work around the lack of a furler. There was now no reason not to continue and though we had lost the best part of a day making the repair, we dived back into the Roaring Forties and had beautiful flat seas all the way to the Kerguelen Islands, which we left to the north. After leaving some icebergs on the distant horizon to the south, we enjoyed a record run across the Indian Ocean. For six days solid, Slattery remarked on how every time he came on watch, the same cloud bank lay ahead. We were making 530 to 550 miles every day so we tracked the weather system ahead until it slowed down and we overtook it.

By the end of the Pacific, however, we were in trouble once more as we got trapped on the wrong side of a static low-pressure system and the seas deteriorated. To make matters worse, the violent slamming of the mainsail started to rip the mainsail track off the mast. The only remedy was to go aloft once again and try to salvage parts and keep the mainsail from flogging itself off the rig completely. Over the space of five days, this happened three times in a row and each time, Scully, Slattery and I climbed into harnesses and swung out of the rig as the boat bashed steadily eastwards.

The job involved backing out each of the bolts holding the track in place on the mast just far enough to get the vice-grips onto to it and twist it out. Each section of track had around thirty bolts and it was a painfully slow process. For some, we'd have to drill the bolt out so a steady stream of batteries and drill bits were sent up and down on halyards from the crew below. We were running out of tools and parts so the cabin was busy with sharpening the bits and grinding the loose bits of track in usable sections. Each section of track that had to be replaced took almost two days and although it was by now extremely rough, the boat pressed on, driven by just the mast and headsail. It was too dangerous to press hard but the record attempt was also at stake. Those directly involved in the repair abandoned the watch system, typical enough in such incidents. The repair was essential because, either way, we had to sail out of this area of ocean that was notorious for breakdowns. Many of us had direct experience – the *Maiden* round-the-world catamaran had dismasted here as had Lawrie Smith's *Silk Cut*, for example. Gerry Roufs had been lost in the Vendeé Globe in this final 1,000-mile approach to the bottom of South America and the narrow passage to the Antarctic Peninsula that halts the passage of the low-pressure systems and creates tough conditions to negotiate.

Our week's work held good and, exhausted a few days later, Slattery and I were especially pleased to pass Cape Horn in daylight and on St Patrick's Day. The worst was behind us and we were ahead of the record, or so we thought. A young tropical storm off the Brazilian coast allowed us a fast run up the South Atlantic and we were set up for the final sprint to the finishing line. The boat was fairly wrecked but we had managed to hold it together. Then the massive pin that held the forward crossbeam to the portside bow started to give way. If it sheared off completely, the two hulls would simply sail apart, without hope of repair. Boatbuilder Mike Beasley swung into action. Cutting apart two plastic containers, which just happened to be the exact diameter of the damaged pin, he created the female mould he would use to create the new pin. With some spare carbon sail battens cut to size and high-density resin, the new pin looked like it had been custom-made in a workshop ashore. Once it had been set we were able to slide it neatly into place and the boat was secure once more.

Despite the high rate of attrition we reached the finish while, behind us, de Kersauson on *Geronimo* was also ahead of Peyron's 2002 record but only by less than a day and behind our pace. Our time of 58 days, 9 hours, 32 minutes and 45 seconds had taken a full week off Peyron's record as ratified by the World Speed Sailing Record Council. But a row over entry fees between Fossett and the Jules Verne organisers meant he never got to lift the trophy. If Fossett cared he barely showed it; he had his record. We had become the fastest people to sail around the planet and Slattery and I returned to Ireland for a big celebration.

Port-la-Forêt, Brittany, 2001: 60-foot Trimaran Circuit

Multihull sailing was an obsession for me. I got back sailing small cats, the Formula 18 and a two-season stint on the Olympic Tornado class as a perfect complement to the other racing. I was easily sailing over 200 days of the year and there were still not enough days in the month. The French multihull circuit and the ORMA 60-foot trimarans attracted crowds of spectators numbered in their tens of thousands everywhere they went, in a way the sport is rarely able to do almost anywhere else in the world.

Karine Fauconnier and I had both started out on the Figaro at the same time but by 2001 she was skipper for the *Sergio Tacchini* team. Her father, Yvon, had previously won the Ostar Single-Handed Transatlantic race, and Karine not only had the ingrained seamanship and skill, but a fierce determination. I joined her for a four-year campaign, mainly as her crew coordinator ashore and either helming or mainsail trimming afloat. From humble beginnings the first year, we later delivered a string of wins or podium places and by the third year were amongst the top-ranked boats of the ORMA multihull fleet. It was the heyday for the class, though much later costs would grow out of control and the fleet became a victim of its own success. But for me, it was a case of being in the right place at the right time; if I had been too young to see the Formula 40 days Paul Standbridge had told me about, now I was where it was at and the dream continued.

Fauconnier entered the 2002 Route du Rhum single-handed transatlantic race from Saint-Malo to Guadeloupe and my role was as her pre-race coach and then shore-based weather routing and navigation support. It was only her second year in this class, but little did she know it was to be a baptism of fire. Two days after leaving Saint-Malo, the fleet was lashed by a big storm and her boat started to break apart. It began when her floater hull broke away, causing the rig to collapse. She declared an emergency and a cargo ship was diverted to the scene. A difficult rescue was performed as Karine first abandoned ship to the life raft and then awkwardly transferred onto the larger vessel. That still left *Sergio Tacchini* abandoned and drifting but within reach of land for a salvage attempt as the on-board tracking still showed the position.

Elsewhere, the fleet of fifteen trimarans was being savaged. Incredibly, no lives were lost. Just three boats completed the course.

Through a Portuguese sailing friend, we managed to locate a deep-sea trawler whose crew was more than happy to sit back and go on a hunting expedition for a yacht instead of the grind of fishing. We left Paris at 11 p.m. and by 4 a.m. had joined the trawler in a fishing port on the west of Madeira and were pounding upwind, the rescue process now well under way. The aftermath of the storm still kicked up a brutal seaway. The last week had been terribly stressful as we been in contact with the boat twenty-four hours a day leading up to and then after the accident.

Despite the Portuguese wine and goat stew on offer we passed on dinner in the mess that night and tried to sleep as the boat pitched and rolled northwards. The following day, thanks to the satellite-tracking beacon, the trimaran – minus one hull – was located; she was in a miserable state. After launching a RIB to pass a tow, the slow journey back to land for the boat to be refitted began. The rebuild of *Sergio Tacchini* was a lengthy process and it was during this downtime that I headed off to join Fossett on *Cheyenne* for the record attempt in the Jules Verne Trophy.

Le Havre, France, 2003

I was back in time to join Fauconnier for our third year of the campaign with the boat refitted to full strength, including some improvements. It was to be my first short-handed transatlantic race and we were quietly confident as we joined thirteen other trimarans as part of the Transat Jacques Vabre for a 5,000-mile double-handed marathon across the Atlantic to Brazil.

Between monohulls and the trimarans, a fleet of thirty-eight boats began the race, although the start was postponed for four days for the multihulls due to gale force conditions. It was decided that the multis would not have to go around Ascension Island and so would take the same direct route as the other boats. The high winds also meant that the race was sailed at a breakneck pace and ended with Franck Cammas and co-skipper Franck Proffit on *Groupama* taking the hat-trick of overall line honours, the class win and a new course record.

We achieved a credible third and it felt good and well deserved. We had put heart and soul into the race from start to finish and had delivered a near faultless performance against the best in the world. Until the final day, the leaders were grouped together and our third place was just under four hours behind first place and had crossed the Atlantic at an average speed of around 16 knots, with the last four days spent reaching at breakneck speeds on one hull all the way to the finishing line in Salvador de Bahia. It was a massive morale boost, especially for Fauconnier who had tried and failed twice before to race across the Atlantic. But there was better yet to come the following year.

Quebec to Saint-Malo, 2004

The 2004 Transat, the original single-handed race, was dominated from the start in Plymouth to the finish in

Boston by maestro Michel Desjoyeaux who skirted ice fields and depressions to win overall. The return race, the 'Quebec to Saint-Malo', is a fully crewed classic staged every four years and I flew to Boston to join boat captain Phillipe 'Pipo' Cairo and his team to deliver the boat to Canada.

We arrived on Quebec's national day, the Fête de St Jean, and a big party was being held on the Plains of Abraham overlooking the St Lawrence river. After ten days at sea it was a shock to find ourselves immersed in the vibrant city. Pipo was from Guadeloupe and I had known him for more than twelve years; he had been aboard the maxi *La Poste* when we had sailed Boston to Quebec the last time. Now exactly twelve years later we were back again, this time on a state-of-the-art trimaran with race-winning potential.

This time, we had a break in our work schedule over two full weeks to explore Quebec, a province where so much of North America's political history was decided and even today is regarded by many as being a unique part of the development of the main Canadian state. Fishermen from Cork were thought to have arrived there in 1536 and immigration has made the Irish the largest ethnic group in Quebec after the French and Canadians. Only a few miles downstream of Quebec city is Grosse Île; the Irish memorial there is a stark reminder of the estimated 3,000 people who died on the island, making it the largest potato famine cemetery outside Ireland. Most passed away in quarantine in 1847 at the peak of immigration during the Great Famine. A massive 500,000 Irish passed through this centre en route to a better life in Canada over 100 years until it was closed in 1932.

As the start day neared, work on board intensified as we all focused on the 2,950-mile course ahead. As part of the build up to the 400th anniversary of Quebec city, the fleet of boats attracted plenty of visitors and interest from the Québécois, including Suzy-Ann Leclerc who had recently completed a sailing course with friends and came to see the 60-foot trimarans. As luck would have it, I was working on the dock as she walked past and a tour of the boat became a tour of the city. Suzy-Ann had been born in Quebec and after school had travelled the west coast and South America before coming home. Any free time I had was spent with her, but finally the days were cut short by the start of the race.

We started in good company, neck and neck with Cammas on *Groupama* as we led the fleet down the St Lawrence River on our 900-mile match-race. After three intense days we reached the ocean and were finally able to break the elastic-like connection to the rest of the fleet and open up a significant lead as the trimarans came into their own, speeding across the Grand Banks, past Cape Race and Newfoundland towards Europe, racking up 500-mile days with apparent ease.

Since the fifteenth century, the Grand Banks had been at the centre of the European and then North American economies until the crucial cod fishing was ultimately brought into decline by overfishing, collapsing in the 1990s and leaving many communities in the surrounding states and countries without an alternative.

Neal McDonald had made a pit stop in the fishing port of St John's, Newfoundland, when a broken rudder ended a transatlantic record attempt on the 93-foot maxi *Stealth*.

After a long day working on the boat the crew had a night off ashore, they went for a few beers and got talking to a large local guy at the bar with whom they exchanged the usual pleasantries.

'So what do people do around here?' enquired Nelly.

'Well, in the summer we fish and we fuck,' came the reply. 'And in the winter, it's too cold to fish . . .'

We left the Newfies of *Talamh an Éisc* to their fishing season and within a week, we were closing on the finishing line and had eked out a 90-mile lead one day out from Saint-Malo. But the pressure was growing from behind and our lead was narrowing. It was a time for calm nerves as a fleet of sixty spectator boats gathered to greet us on the warm summer evening, and we were escorted to the lock gates outside of the fortified city of Saint-Malo.

We became the sixth winners of the race and though we missed the course record by just thirty-six minutes, we were ecstatic that we hadn't been robbed of our deserved win at the finish. Barely twenty-six minutes later, Cammas on *Groupama* came in second, followed by Desjoyeaux on *Géant* in third. Thomas Coville's *Sodebo* joined them in fourth place; all three were separated by less than ten minutes.

Shortly after our arrival, Suzy-Ann came to France and we celebrated our win with the team in the old city of Saint-Malo. The beers flowed and the rum came out as we wended our way from bar to bar through the medieval streets of the famous town. Three months later, Suzy-Ann left her job in Quebec and moved across the ocean to live in Port-la-Fôret.

8

The World Turned Upside Down

Transat Jacque Vabre: Le Havre to Brazil, 2005

If Alain Gautier was worried, his expression revealed little of it. Instead, a bemused look crossed his weathered face as he matched our speed, boat for boat; he was on our team RIB while Armel Le Cléac'h and I were streaking away from the start line of the double-handed Transat Jacques Vabre off Le Havre on *Foncia*, a 60-foot trimaran. Astern, a crowd of more than 100,000 people watched our rapid progress from the short spectacle course away to the horizon.

A veteran French skipper with over half a million ocean miles that made him a household name in his native country and a legend throughout the world of sailing, Gautier could hardly have been better pleased to see his crew lead the 36-strong fleet to the first mark of this transatlantic epic race. After months of training and preparation, sponsorship investment awaiting its return and always in the background, the fine balance between risk and reward from man pitted against nature, the stakes were as high as ever. Except that now he was not on board and was instead hanging on to the RIB while Armel and I powered off on his boat, cautiously throwing half-glances astern to see if our lead was holding against the monohulls and other 60-foot trimarans strung out on this fast leg to the turning mark leading us into open ocean.

As a Breton, Armel shared with me a common Celtic upbringing and resolve, and we quickly sailed to the front of the pack, determined not to relinquish that place without a fight. Ten years younger than me, Armel was one of the top up-and-coming sailors in the French offshore sailing world. He had come second in the gruelling Vendée Globe race that was an incredible result and testimony to the intelligent race he had sailed, opting not to take risks but sail conservatively and protect his ability to stay in the race rather than be forced out due to gear failure or injury. We had met when he was the weather routeur for our Transat Jacques Vabre campaign with Karine Fauconnier but it was his own victory in the Figaro race, when he beat Gautier by just three seconds, that persuaded the *Foncia* team to sign him on as their new skipper. Eventually, Gautier's RIB struggled to keep pace with *Foncia*, which revelled in the quick, reaching conditions of the freshening breeze. Riding high above the waves, we could look down into the inflatable where our boat's former skipper, now turned project manager, was determined to escort us, keeping the bond between sailing crew and shore team intact for as long as possible before leaving us to our own devices. From the final sponsor duties the night before to seeing us safely off the dock, this was as much their moment as ours, the time that the two sides of the project are equalised and total responsibility passes on to the sailing crew's shoulders. Ended at last was the period of madcap schedules, checklists, technical and logistical issues, each demanding to be balanced. Keeping that intensity on the sane side of the equation meant leaving time for some light stretching, running or swimming in the final few days as well as time with family and then holding pace with media and event demands.

For Suzy-Ann, it was no longer a new experience, though this was our biggest race to date and her final, fleeting glimpse would be as a guest on a sponsor boat at the starting line. However, the reality of living this life for the family ashore is far from glamorous and Suzy-Ann's commitment was now as much an important part of my success as any other aspect of the racing.

As we passed the turning buoy, our boat speed increased beyond the limit for the five shore-team members on the RIB and they prepared to turn for home, their job now done after putting their all into getting the project to this stage. But at that point of the last goodbye to everything land-based, it is all-smiling 'big bananas', no need for shouting or messages; this is a family-type moment when spoken words are unnecessary. It is the briefest flash of collective feeling when the huge stress leading up to the start is suddenly eased with the private thought, 'this *is it,* boys: we're doing it, we're in the lead!'

Somewhere off Saint-Malo, a year later

Every sporting discipline seems to have its own unique characters who often become known as mavericks, naturals, gifted and just plain lucky. Attaching such tag onto Alain Gautier, or any ocean-going sailor for that matter, is ill advised as the variables involved are certain either to disappoint or exceed such expectations. While it is their adventures and exploits that form the stuff of legends, the true test can only be made in person. A year later, on a delivery trip bringing *Foncia* to Saint-Malo for the start of the Route du Rhum – the holy grail of Transatlantic races – I saw first hand how his reputation was earned.

We were under pressure to reach port before the dock gates were closed for the tide or we would be forced to spend the night outside the harbour until early morning. It was a relaxed, easy-going trip but we were sailing fast as time was against us, even though we were already picking our way through fairly hazardous waters, known for shallows and rocks that offer risk-takers a maritime version of Russian roulette.

Now, Alain isn't the type to let such trivial things as deadlines get the better of him. And when most people have already taken in a couple of reefs, Alain is often still to be to be found with full main and flying hulls higher than the rest. As night started closing in on the final approach to Saint-Malo, I was at the helm when Philippe popped his head out from the cabin where Alain was seated at the nav. station.

'Alain wants you to luff up thirty degrees,' was the short instruction to sail closer to the wind direction.

We were already at half-tide and all around us were the jagged edges of rocks that hinted at far worse beneath the surface, which couldn't be easily spotted. The northwest channel was easily the safest entrance, especially as this was a delivery trip ahead of a major race.

'We're already in the channel,' I said, hoping that such information wouldn't be taken as criticism.

'Yeah, but Alain wants you to luff thirty,' said Philippe, relieving me with the certain knowledge that our skipper was more than happy with our position.

Within minutes, a series of course alterations followed: up five, down ten, down five, up ten . . . all the time carrying us at more than ten knots over an area that would be dry and rock-strewn at low water, until we crossed the bar and safely docked in Saint-Malo. Later, we met the harbourmaster who had tracked our progress by radar in the expectation of drama. When he heard our boat name, it was as if a wager had been settled in his favour.

'Ah, so it WAS *Foncia* coming through the south passage – that explains it,' he half-shouted, delighted with the news and not at all bothered by the risk involved.

But although Gautier's influence remains huge, his humanity and ability to relate to people at a normal level prevents him becoming an idol. He remains a discreet person, preferring to keep a low profile when possible and is easily one of the most approachable skippers, much like Ellen MacArthur; like her, he simply loves being at sea.

It is a huge advantage to work with different people: you see various styles of work, managing and dealing with people, and problem solving. You have to experience this and see what works and what does not and then accept that there is only so much you can change in yourself. You try and remember 'I'm still my own person' and that at the end of the day we all have our own ways of sailing, trimming, communicating with people and the way we run our lives.

Back to Le Havre, 2005: Race Start

Any resident of northwest Europe's frontier, from Brittany and all around Ireland to Scotland and Scandinavia, is all too familiar with an established annual weather pattern. From early autumn onwards, wind and rain seem to pelt down with almost rhythmic regularity.

The birthplace for these systems lies on the western side of the North Atlantic Ocean close to the edge of the United States mainland from around the Great Lakes to Cape Hatteras and Nova Scotia. In this region, two distinctly different air masses – one with cold dry air from the Arctic north and the other with warm moist air from the south are divided by the oscillating jet stream. As the young depressions form, both air masses meet to create a front, like a stand-off between two great armies. Shortly after birth, the depressions rapidly begin their journey eastwards, passing over Nova Scotia and the Grand Banks, the wind and sea state building in strength and intensity. Steered by the jet stream, with a slingshot effect they cross the Atlantic around the northern edge of the semi-permanent Azores High arriving with full force on the doorstep of Europe's northwestern coasts.

Three days prior to Armel and me starting the Transat Jacques Vabre on Saturday 6 November 2005, a deep low-pressure system of 950 mb crossed the coast of Newfoundland. It was following the path of a similar system a few days earlier that had now matured into a North Atlantic gale, indicating that the autumn train of depressions was in full swing. As the new system gathered pace on its route towards Iceland, a secondary low was cast off its weakest area at the southern sector. Following the track of the warm Gulf Stream and strengthened on its four-day journey, a 50-knot storm was to be unleashed on the western approaches and its predicted track neatly crossed over the early stage of the race course in the notorious Bay of Biscay.

In general, North Atlantic weather depressions feature two fronts – first warm then cold, the outcome of the stand-off between the two air masses earlier. From days beforehand, when the depression can be observed forming in the west on weather charts, it is possible to predict with surprising accuracy their likely path, broadly estimate their arrival time and plan to deal with the vicious conditions they can deliver.

Reading the weather and knowing the signs are critical. Before the race start, Armel and I knew what to expect and had planned a conservative approach to the first phase. As this was the most significant weather we could expect before getting into the warmer latitudes nearer Africa, we planned to cross the cold front as far south as possible in the hope of allowing the worst of the weather to pass us to the north. And, if we timed it correctly, we would have flatter seas and faster conditions as a result. We expected a significant shift in wind direction from southwest to northwest when the front arrived and it was vital to be set up with reduced sail area before that happened, not least because it would occur in the middle of the night.

◄◦►

Armel and I were getting on well, pleased with our position, albeit pretty tired from keeping the pace on after two nights at sea. We had planned every hour of the race well in advance and saw each other only as we swapped watch for rest and food when we also reviewed our progress. Although fatigued, we were quietly confident that the race would settle down and a rhythm of sorts would become the norm on board.

The type of comfort on offer was limited. On *Foncia*'s centre hull, a narrow companionway led through a very narrow hatch from the cockpit into the cabin. Immediately inside, a single bunk lay between the hatch and the navigation station that was flanked by a single burner for cooking up our freeze-dried meals.

Our nav. station comprised a small desk and a computer monitor powered by two PCs that ran our various systems: boat data from various sensors such as wind speed, depth, compass, navigation systems, such as electronic charts that had overlays of latest weather data, boat performance targets from our extensive tests using different sail combinations in various wind ranges, radar and autopilot; and our weather-routing software that combined all the elements of information to provide a shortlist of options to base our decisions on.

While some races allow outside assistance such as expert weather routing on call, others do not allow any. The Transat Jacques Vabre permitted limited external data in the form of weather data electronic GRIB files to be downloaded using satcoms, but interpretation by a meteorologist was banned.

Our routine comprised 60 per cent helming duties and

some deck work, 20 per cent of the time supposedly devoted to rest and eating, with the remainder spent in front of the screen. Routine maintenance was carried out in addition to critical rig checks every morning on the 90-foot wing-mast but as the weather worsened, only essential items were carried out while a backlog accumulated for the first opportunity during calmer conditions.

The crew coming off watch would usually start by downloading the latest data and, while this was in progress, put the kettle on. Downloads would be the weather GRIBs and also regular skeds showing the positions of the other boats. If there was nothing to download, the progress of the last few hours would be reviewed to help assess performance ahead of the next planning discussion and whether a change of strategy was needed.

After all that, plus the watch just completed, rest would be the priority and, regardless of the hull movement, exhaustion virtually guaranteed sleep. A solid bulkhead forward divided the living quarters from another unused space forward that was accessible only via a deck hatch. Moving aft from the bunk, a space beneath the cockpit deckhead was used for stacking supplies and other weighty items such as spares and sails. A bucket served as the toilet facility; creature comforts aboard a racing trimaran means finding space between equipment and sails. The deck of the cabin also had a watertight hatch leading straight down, for use in the worst emergency possible: capsize.

On deck, if the routine was working well, there was little to do other than helm the boat. From the centre-hull cockpit, two arms on both sides led out to the hulls that were simply void spaces but essential for achieving the near-flight capabilities of the trimaran. On both wing-hulls, twin steering positions were the nerve centre of the watch, depending on which tack the boat was sailing.

A comfortable bucket seat beside the steering tiller was sheltered from the worst seas by a wave guard. Instruments grouped together fed essential information to the driver who constantly balanced the data with the feel of the boat's trim. A foot-operated button was ready to 'dump' the hydraulic mainsail sheet if the boat was suddenly overpowered; smaller adjustments could be made manually by the small hand-winch beside the seat. And rather than leave the boat on the trusty but unintuitive autopilot, major adjustments to the boat's set-up, such as sail changes or bigger trims, were left to the changeover of the watch. The helmsman had to juggle these controls while bracing against the movement of the tri and figure how to avoid dropping the boat into especially steep waves, a task that required good concentration – even more so at night when darkness conspired with driving spray to blind any vision of the seas ahead. From time to time, alone on deck and also keeping watch for hazards such as other vessels, the helm would have to manage to look beneath the mainsail boom to spot any traffic and, at night, navigation lights indicating other vessels' movements. When sailing solo or short-handed, it is essential to understand what is happening so a hand-bearing compass is used to calculate whether a risk of collision exists. Over a five- to ten- minute period, a constant bearing and closing distance to a target would confirm such a risk, but in the fast trimarans, the simplest avoidance measure would be to slow down until the risk passes; trying major manoeuvres is hugely time-consuming while also upsetting the rhythm on board and progress in the race.

Nevertheless, in case of an urgent situation, we had a call-button system on board with a button beside the helm position relayed to the bunk in the cabin and a simple code. One buzz: 'can you pop up on deck for a minute for something routine?'; two buzzes: 'get on your foul-weather gear and come on deck'; three buzzes (and more): 'emergency: get on deck now!'

Still ahead of the bad weather, the sailing conditions were beautiful. Bright sunshine reflected off long, glassy swells as we sped upwind through the Chanel du Four at boat speeds of between 18 and 20 knots in less than 15 knots of wind, heading out into the Bay of Biscay.

Aside from the overall goal of winning the race, our short-term aim was to get into our own rhythm with our craft. Ultimately, on any vessel it is the boat and the weather conditions that decide what we can and cannot do; moving around a racing yacht at sea and at speed is a tricky affair. And when it is a trimaran, the complexity simply increases as the speed rises.

As the wind picks up, reducing sail becomes essential and a well-practised method comes into its own. Making the decision to change up or down sail will have evolved over a series of updates as the watch changes. Generally, our system was the crew going off watch would download the latest weather files and begin planning the coming hours. On the next watch, the plan would become more detailed and on the third change, a discussion would confirm the strategy for the hours ahead, taking all factors into account, all the while bearing in mind the regular skeds that report the fleet's position and performance.

It is vital to maintain consistency because the moment that is lost is when errors start to happen, with major gear breakage and capsize being our two nightmare scenarios. To prevent that happening, planning ahead and anticipation of outcomes is essential and we had systems for everything we could think of, even printing off the most important plans and sticking them to the cabin beside the nav. station. We simply could not afford to get anything wrong or allow margin for error: 'if you fuck up, you'll fall over,' we used to repeat.

As we were heading upwind, to make sail changes we would have to bear away downwind so that we could furl the headsails and, as these were bigger and therefore more difficult to handle, we would try to reduce these first by daylight. Taking in reefs or 'slabs' of the mainsail was an easier process and, provided we took care to tie them properly, we could avoid water building up in the folds, which damages the sail material. Though physically demanding, the process itself was quite straightforward. First, we would prepare all the lines and winches we would need. Next, we would bear away to reduce the pressure on the sails and the autopilot would be switched on as both crew would jump on the grinder winch to furl the huge 'Solent' genoa headsail. Then a staysail would be set, hanked on to its own stay running from the mast to the deck of the centre-hull and hoisted from its sail bag, which was clipped on permanently. We also had a 'down-fucker' system so that one crew could control this sail if it needed to be quickly dropped. If conditions became really strong, we also had an 'ORC' storm jib which was hanked on with sheets attached and ready to used almost instantly.

The problem is that bearing away from the wind and your optimum course means taking a big hit to your race position straight away. Nevertheless, it still leaves you better set up when the new wind arrives and with the reassurance that the competition must do the same as well.

We managed to change sails half an hour before Michel Desjoyeaux on *Geánt* did each time so that meant gradually pulling ahead, leaving *Geánt* to leeward. Franck Cammas on *Groupama* had tacked earlier and was slightly ahead of us in the west but still further north. The three of us led the fleet out into the Atlantic towards the front in the building breeze.

With the freshening winds, the boat was starting to slam and was affected by the conditions; the difference between a multihull and a monohull was very evident. A single-hulled yacht spends more time in the water and, especially with modern race boats, endures a lot of slamming. A trimaran is drier in moderate conditions as the object is to keep the boat flying a-hull – keeping just one of the three hulls in the water and the boat slightly heeled, but not too much so or capsize becomes likely. Keeping the boat 'flying' and going fast gets complicated at night because if a multihull has too little sail up the boat goes flat in the water and slams more. Another difference from a single-hulled yacht is that a multihull also tends to have movement in the 'platform' between hulls that helps to dampen slamming. A different motion called 'racking' occurs when the leeward hull digs into the waves; the windward hull moves forward until the leeward hull comes out of the wave and catches up causing a twisting type movement of acceleration and deceleration almost simultaneously.

From the weather information coming in, we knew we had about eighteen hours of hard sailing ahead to get past the worst of the weather, which we accepted: in certain parts of a race, we might normally push a little harder perhaps to get through to more favourable conditions sooner. You try to sail at 100 per cent all the time but especially at the early stages of a short transatlantic race, when the decisions you make early on will be the ones you have to live with later.

Racing across this ocean, there are typically between three and five clear decision-making points of whether to gybe or make major course alterations, and the more of these we got right, the better our chances of winning. Between each major decision, our overall finishing place would depend on our day-to-day performance and, in spite of the speed of the trimarans, the differences between fast and much faster are so big that making every manoeuvre routinely smooth is essential.

But we were as well set up as we could ever be and we were simply helming the whole time now, to keep the boat going through the waves while trying to keep as much of the centre hull as possible out of the waves. The trick is not to heel the boat too much as the risk of capsize only increases. This process just gets harder in bigger waves and so bearing away from the optimum course is sometimes needed as well. This balancing act is decided by having the right amount of sail up and using the daggerboard in the leeward and centre hulls to reduce the lifting moment – the more daggerboard that is down, the more lateral resistance is caused and the boat flies a-hull more. By taking the daggerboard up, the tendency is reduced, which is more important as the waves get bigger.

We had started out intending to have a watch system of two hours on, two hours off. But after an intense two days at sea, we were already down to one on, one off, though we tried to stay going longer and give the crewmate a decent break. But this proved impossible due to fatigue and the proximity of the other boats. We started thinking about the final reduction of sail in anticipation of the weather front that was likely to strike overnight.

Although concentrating on the race, at the same time we were watching for the warning of the active front bringing rain and squally, unmanageable winds. The wind shift is the sign and a speedy response would avoid disaster. As usual, our detailed pre-race planning would be invaluable. The standard approach is to reduce sail by reefing the mainsail and have a hand ready to ease the sheets as the wind quickly accelerates. It is a race within a race to beat nature's arrival by readying the boat and it soon becomes instinctive despite the lack of precise predictability of the gale force gusts. Yet we were going according to plan and feeling comfortable, albeit a little tired.

As the sun set for the third night at sea a strange feeling came over me. The sea state was worsening but not beyond previous experiences and not to anything threatening. Puzzled, I tried to figure out what was bothering me when a convulsion in my gut spewed my precious dinner across the deck and away with the wind. Seasickness is an unfamiliar enemy of mine and its brief arrival would have been recognised by a superstitious sailor as the portent it was for the hours ahead.

At 2 a.m., we changed watch. We had three reefs in the mainsail and the storm jib was already set. It was rough – 5- to 6-metre swells topped by chop – though the sea state was not dangerous or unassailable as the depression had not really had a chance to whip up a full seaway – yet. Typically, when the sou'westerly ahead of the cold front of a depression blows, the wave train follows this direction. But when the wind switches to the northwest, a second wave train is created from this direction and on top of the existing seaway, and so can create a potentially dangerous cross-wave.

We had 30 to 40 knots of wind, a full gale, though we were set up for the 50-knot storm that we were sure was ahead; our aim was to stay comfortable and avoid a survival situation. We were now down to minimal sail, the prudent approach and no more last-minute trekking in darkness across the bouncy netting between the hulls trying to gather sails and sheets.

So we were happy, tipping along nicely. As we prepared to swap over at the helm, the wind eased to around 25 knots. I handed over the helm to Armel and moved across the platform towards the centre hull. In that instant, the wind flicked by 40 degrees, not to the northwest as expected, but to the south. Almost as quickly, the wind speed shot back up to gale force and we were overpowered. I lunged for the cockpit, eased the last of the mainsheet traveller then with a sick feeling in the pit of my stomach grabbed the winch pedestal and hung on as the boat began to heel dangerously. It was too late to do anything else, too late to reach the shelter of the cabin and far too late to discuss what was happening – we were already capsizing and our world was turned upside down.

A searing pain shot through my shoulder as water surged around me. I was pushed beneath the waves by equipment and sails falling over me, as well as a 60-foot trimaran the size of a tennis court, which landed next, pushing all the loose gear and myself underwater. The boom pinned me against a winch that knocked out my last bit of breath. Darkness everywhere – night-time, submerged under deck and gear, in cold water – and all the while trying to survive, feeling around trying to find my bearings and figure where to swim free of the threatening mess. The concept of time changed and my thoughts were clear, but as my brain started to ask for oxygen the clock started ticking again and panic started to build. It was crucial to control it. Automatically, I turned face up and tried to swim and crawl to the back of the boat where clinging onto the trampoline netting allowed one brief gasp of air as the hull rose up on the swells and clear of the waves before submerging me once more. The final hurdle was to crawl over the lifelines upside down and swing clear to grab onto the upturned hull. It was the 'all or nothing' moment that we had talked about, planned for, dreamt about and hoped would never arrive. Death would have been inevitable had it not been for our prior preparation.

Armel had managed to escape injury in the capsize. In the darkness he had been thrown clear of the boat but was able to swim back and climb aboard. He barely had time to begin searching for me when I popped up at the stern. It was only when he started to haul me up that we realised I couldn't move my arm and the agony of a dislocated shoulder took hold. Slowly, he worked me into a position where I could help him heave me on board and I was able to crawl back to the escape hatch and back inside to the relative safety of the upturned cabin in the central hull. We were already dressed in our survival suits from our preparations for crossing the front but I was awash, sitting on the cabin deckhead. I lay almost helpless, trying to avoid any movement that might set off the grating sound in my shoulder and a fresh bout of pain while also wedging myself against the rise and crashing fall of the boat in the swell. The survival suit had been damaged and was letting in water; now the cold was slowly taking hold and I started to shake.

Armel dug our Iridium satphone out of the grab bag and was soon in contact with the shore team, reporting our situation. At first, there was no panic, no stress, just acceptance of what had happened and knowing nothing could reverse it. The priority now was survival until rescue, however long that might take.

As Alain began the process of contacting the race organisers and French authorities, we were left to contemplate our situation and the race that had ended. I was swamped by a feeling of disappointment and frustration. It was easy to make room for recriminations; we had complete confidence that our boat was sound and in no danger of sinking so we were safe. For sure, our race was over and the months of planning were now wasted.

What had happened? Instead of a 40-degree shift heralding the arrival of the cold front, a relative lull can also be a precursor to the bigger shift. It was simply timing, bad luck that it happened exactly as we were distracted with swapping over the watch and settling into the new routine. Had it been a minute earlier or later then either of us could have booted the foot-switch that would have instantly depowered the mainsail. Had we been clipped on with safety harnesses, as we might well have been on a monohull, we would probably not have survived since unclipping the lines would have been next to impossible in a full multihull capsize situation. We had nobody to blame but ourselves yet we had nothing to blame ourselves for: the outcome did not reflect the way we had prepared nor the way we had sailed. For years to come, this would be the biggest disappointment of my sailing life, not just because we had capsized someone else's boat but because we had not realised our potential. We had been cheated.

Hours later, in daylight once more and after regular updates via the satphone to ascertain that our situation had not worsened and to provide information for the team to salvage *Foncia* later on, a French naval helicopter arrived overhead. We crawled through the escape hatch one last time and into the rescue basket to be winched to safety. We joined brothers Steve and Yvan Ravussin from the *Orange* trimaran who had also just been rescued and we were all flown ashore to hospital in Brest.

The race had continued but *Groupama, Sodebo* and *Fila* were also to suffer similar events; Franck Proffit from *Groupama* also ended up in hospital with a crushed thorax and water in his lungs after being ejected into the front beam during a full pitchpole that saw the boat finish upside down just south of Madeira. Shocked by the sudden turn of events that brought home the risks the sport involved, Suzy-Ann came to visit me and, after a overnight stay, I was discharged. Ironically, the dislocation had reset itself during the rescue hoist to the helicopter and needed minimal medical attention. Better still, after a short period of rest and physiotherapy, there was nothing to stop me from going sailing again three weeks later: the next race was beckoning. But the memory lived on. We had abandoned ship.

9

Non-stop, Never Give Up

Mid-Atlantic, 2007

Water sloshed around my feet as Suzy-Ann and I talked on the satphone, catching up on her day's news in the final weeks counting down to the arrival of our first child. Sailing conditions off the east coast of the United States were relatively benign for me while the arrival of Suzy-Ann's mother in Lorient the previous day was reassurance that she would not be alone until I arrived home two weeks before the expected birth.

Jean-Pierre Dick was on deck, his imposing size squeezed into the helmsman seat, steering *Paprec Virbac*, the 60-foot monohull, as we sailed from Panama to Halifax. It was our qualifier passage and shake-down sail in preparation for the Barcelona World Race. We had left the Caribbean and the balmy trade winds behind and were now three days from Halifax where our plan was that I would step off the boat and return to France and Suzy-Ann.

Although the chat was good and the news was all positive, the waves crashing over the deck could not account for the amount of water washing around the bilge and my feet so I was quite distracted. Something was wrong. We ended our call and I began hunting for the source of the water. Quickly enough, it was clear one of our through-hull fittings for the hydraulic canting system for the keel was leaking – badly. We set up a chain of buckets, bailing the bottom of the boat around the bilge and gradually the water level started returning to normal. The phone rang at the nav. station and J. P. went aft to answer the call.

'Damian, it's Suzy-Ann,' he called.

'Tell her I'll call her back in a while.'

'No, you'd better take this. Something about water . . .'

'Sure, I know all about water, haven't we got gallons of it here for the last hour,' I said, just as the penny dropped. On the other side of the Atlantic, a drama of a different kind had started. We could not sail to Nova Scotia any faster nor would our baby delay arriving in time for me to fly home. We sailed into Halifax three days later and while waiting for the next flight out, I spent a day helping J. P. rig the boat for single-handed mode before I jumped on a plane back to Paris and then to Quimper in time to collect Suzy-Ann from hospital.

Our son Oisín's early arrival got me off the hook for being in the delivery room and, while motherhood seemed natural for Suzy-Ann, the most important and rewarding part of my life was starting. The responsibility was fabulous and daunting as I now had to start growing into the role of parent. A new-found caution of sorts started. I would not have been reckless before Oisín's arrival but, had I been, I would now be less so. In fact, it may have even improved my performance as the need to take fewer risks sharpens judgement. Winning at sea is still important but my new family at home is by far the higher priority. It is something that can be seen on many ocean racing crews where gentle comments such as reminders to don harnesses and clip on come from a new perspective.

Preparation for the Barcelona World Race

This entry for the inaugural Barcelona World Race in 2007 was more than a year in preparation and came about just after I had finished the 2006 Volvo Ocean Race with *Ericsson* in July of that year. I had not taken time off but had gone straight on to race with my *Ericsson* crewmate Magnus Woxen on a small catamaran in the Swedish Archipelago Raid, ten days non-stop, sailing and paddling day and night, with the sun dipping below the horizon for only a few hours that far north. Little to no sleep, but we won, a nice consolation for what had been a frustrating Volvo race.

Suzy-Ann had stayed on with me in Sweden for a well-deserved holiday as we had both worked hard during the Volvo. We cruised in the islands on a friend's boat and in the final days, I chanced my arm and proposed, and to my relief and joy she accepted. We moved back to Lorient in Brittany where I began working with Franck Cammas who was preparing a Jules Verne record attempt with his giant *Groupama 3* trimaran but a chance meeting with Jean-

Pierre Dick at the Paris Boat Show in December resulted in a fresh opportunity: J. P. had still to decide on his co-skipper for his new Open 60-footer *Paprec Virbac* for the two-handed Barcelona World Race. We knew each other well as I had been navigator for him during the Tour de France à la Voile in 2001. This new project would be crewed by only two – both co-skippers and racing non-stop around the world. It was too good a chance to refuse. This was a new race that was starting to attract a lot of interest, especially amongst the solo and short-handed sector of the sport.

At over 6 feet J. P. is an imposing person, but on first encounter this is quickly matched by his gentle, almost aloof manner, which hides a cold, steely determination and deep resources of endurance. From a rich French family, his late father had passed on his love of sailing and J. P. had cast aside his training as a vet to forge his own path up through the echelons of French ocean sailing. He now had a reputation as a serious contender, especially in double-handed racing. This time, I did change project, giving my apologies to Cammas while definitely not wanting to burn any bridges, and I joined J. P.

We agreed our programme and initially I spent a lot of time in Ireland with my friend John McKenna from Dublin, who was kindly seconded to our project by Mark Turner at OC Events, to hunt for any sponsorship we could find at home. We pitched the idea of an Irish entry or even a co-flagged entry widely but drew no results so the project remained French-flagged with me as co-skipper. The potential and the following that the race was to develop was totally underestimated: it was a missed opportunity for commercial sponsors. While the build was being completed in New Zealand, Suzy-Ann and I flew to Quebec where we got married. With friends from Kerry and her family from Canada, we had a far too short week of skiing and dog-sledding before our wedding. Midwinter is definitely off-season for traditional Canadian weddings and as a few of the lads stepped off the plane from Ireland into minus 25 degrees Celsius wearing only T-shirts, a rapid upgrading of wardrobes took place.

From Quebec and without having a honeymoon – a thorny issue that remains outstanding – I flew to New Zealand to join J. P. in commissioning the new boat. We had planned to sail the boat back to Europe via Cape Horn but delays tuning the rig meant the boat would return with a full crew sailing with J. P. while I went back to Suzy-Ann after a two-month absence. When I returned to the boat in Panama City, J. P. and I obtained the extensive paperwork needed to transit the canal. We entered just behind a large container vessel but our engine failed before the dock gates closed and the wash of the larger vessel flushed us out of the canal. The whole transit process had to be started again but we eventually passed through and began our qualification passage through the idyllic sailing waters of the Caribbean Sea and into the Atlantic and the Gulf Stream conveyor belt northwards towards Canada.

By the time Oisín was born at the end of May, we had already sailed more miles together on *Paprec Virbac* than the other skippers despite the tight schedule we were on before the start of the race just five months later. But if the pressure was on for our qualification passage, on arrival in

France a routine refit and survey of our keel discovered critical fractures in the keel that were probably a result of the casting process when impurities were missed in the pouring of the molten lead. A big debate followed between team headquarters in France and the keel fabricators in New Zealand that eventually saw a new fin poured and shipped to us. We had to suspend our training plans, including the Round Britain and Ireland Race, as we used the time to plan every minute detail of the intense three-month race ahead of us.

Any voyage around the world – 23,000 nautical miles for a typical non-stop course or up to 40,000 miles for a Volvo Ocean Race with its stopover ports – requires massive amounts of preparation. And once under way, this preparation is the difference between completing a circumnavigation and pulling out after a few weeks or even days. Winning is the potential result of the work done before the start.

Barcelona World Race 2007 – Race Log

Log I

11 November 2007: the start from Barcelona and the dash southwards past the Balearics towards Gibraltar and the open Atlantic Ocean.

We're finally under way after months of preparation and expectation. It's great to be off the dock and begin the adventure that is this mammoth race, the Barcelona World Race, in which just J. P. Dick and I will pit ourselves against the fleet of eight other two-handed crews. And non-stop too.

Our team of ten shore crew are now looking to the two of us to deliver on all our hard work though it will be a while yet before we can really demonstrate our new Open 60-footer's capability.

Paprec Virbac is state of the art and we've been tweaking her since she was launched in New Zealand last February. Since then we've sailed halfway around the world, trialling every aspect of the boat and sails and especially the new trim-tabs, which are the biggest ever used on a racing boat.

The recent spate of mast breakages on other Open 60s is a concern, for sure, but so far we've had no issues with our rig after all the intensive testing. Over the summer, we fitted a new keel so we're reassured on that front.

Overall, our preparations have served us well so we can focus solely on the race ahead, which will be a new experience for me. Although this circumnavigation is my seventh time to race around the planet, in one sense it's a first as I've just left my wife, Suzy-Ann, on the dock with Oisín who was born just five months ago. This is going to be strange, watching him grow by video and email.

Suzy-Ann and I have planned for this since February. We took a quick week off in the mountains before the start of race and we'll both just lead our own lives for the next three months, staying in touch, hopefully three times a week, which will help me to switch off from the intensity of racing.

Now I realise how difficult it has been for my crewmates on previous campaigns who have had to leave their families behind and I appreciate even more what they achieved. Overall it's going to be a new reason to be motivated. J. P.

and I have discussed and planned for all possible dramas. We've really connected well and complement one another. He's been around once before, in the last Vendée Globe [single-handed, non-stop] and he placed sixth, which is pretty impressive.

But for the pair of us this week, just getting out of the Med with light winds will be a job in itself. We're expecting light airs until Tuesday at least and so our options boil down to diving south to Ibiza to position for the new wind on Tuesday or hug the coast, a more direct route, in the hope of finding night breezes.

We have to limit any potential losses until we reach the Atlantic so keeping up in the leading pack is the basis of our strategy until we get through the Straits of Gibraltar. It's fairly straightforward till then but as the weekend beckons, the pressure will really start to build on us as we start the mad dash to the Canary Islands and first scoring gate of the race. As we sailed past Malaga, I phoned my dad to say hello to him; he's now living there in the Axarquía Hills with his new family.

North Atlantic: Cape Verde Islands, 14° 55' N 23° 31' W

At just 570 kilometres from the Senegalese coast, the Cape Verde Islands are much closer to Africa though benefitting from a milder climate. The significant archipelago of ten islands was inhabited only in the fifteenth century and became a strategic mid-Atlantic maritime staging post for centuries, especially for the slave trade. In the modern era, tourism has made a slow impact on the islands with an established reputation as a centre for wave sailing.

Log 2

25 November 2007: tracking southwards, past the Cape Verde Islands off West Africa and looking for the best place to cross the equator. At this stage, *Paprec Virbac* had led the race out of the Mediterranean through both the scoring gates at Gibraltar and Gran Canaria.

Today is make or break. All our hard work could go up in smoke and our tactics in the next stage of the race really depend on whether we have made the right call in our choice for tackling the infamous doldrums region just north of the equator.

Since passing through the Canaries one week ago today, we have managed to hold and even extend our lead against the chasing pack. At one point, we had almost 100 miles on Vincent Riou and Seb Josse on *PRB* who have stuck to us like glue in second place, waiting for our first mistake to take advantage.

Our choice at Gran Canaria was either to duck out to the west or hug the African coast and head south. The usually reliable trade winds were absent with a low-pressure system in their place. We almost went west but in the end opted to tack southwards. Either seemed to have been a fair call as Roland Jourdain and Jean-Luc Nélias on *Veolia Environnement* picked up to third place by going west. But we maintained our lead and that's what counts for us.

Until we reached the Cape Verde Islands, cutting between these saw our lead drop once again as we gybed eight times in a single night. We probably sailed a few extra miles here but ultimately we were able to open ground on

PRB though shaking them off completely is a tough challenge. From the Cape Verdes, we've been locked into an intense race to get as far west as possible to get set up for the doldrums crossing. So far, this region has been relatively stable and while we expect the fleet to gain on us as we slow down, we're hoping to get through quickly and pick up the new trade winds on the other side.

For the last three days before reaching the doldrums region, we have been surfing downwind at speeds of more than 20 knots. Exhilarating sailing, for sure, but this has placed massive demands on both of us physically as the autopilot can't handle this angle so we're hand-steering constantly. My right arm is aching and my legs are cramped but at least we're able to maintain a three hours on, three hours off watch system.

On Saturday, we spent most of the afternoon getting the boat set up for crossing the doldrums where we must prepare for sudden changes that could see us get from zero to 35 knots of wind in the squalls and for the erratic conditions that make up the Intertropical Convergence Zone.

So far our only repair has been to a torn kite and we want to keep it this way for as long as possible.

Once we're through, hopefully today, we can head straight for the Brazilian island of Fernando de Noronha, our next scoring gate. After that, we welcome our 'third helmsman' back for a long reach southwards towards the Southern Ocean and an opportunity to climb the rig for an inspection and really get settled for the biggest challenge that lies ahead.

But we've slowed now, down from 17 knots to just 7, while the others are watching our progress on the two-hourly position reports, so they could yet sail around us. This could still prove to be a 240-mile stage to restart the entire race at the equator.

Log 3

2 December 2007: three full weeks out and now in the South Atlantic; we've been leading most of the time but the question remains: for how long?

This is it; countdown mode once again – but after three weeks into this 25,000 mile contest. By next weekend we will have reached the Southern Ocean, probably the most inhospitable region of the planet and certainly the loneliest. Within days, we will have left the Tranquil Twenties and engaged with the Roaring Forties for our circumnavigation of Antarctica.

Our dash down the South Atlantic since crossing the equator has seen a lot happen within the fleet of nine Open 60-footers. Thankfully, the *Paprec Virbac* crew have maintained our position at the head of the fleet and with a tit-for-tat duel with *PRB* that has seen us swap the overall lead between both boats.

We got our equator strategy a bit wrong when we gybed too early, having been in the lead. Our constant rivals, Vincent Riou and Seb Josse on *PRB*, left it later than us, went further west and as a result had a great crossing of the doldrums, barely losing any boat speed, which resulted in a 30-mile lead for them.

Since then, we've been sailing quickly and have hauled them back in and got into the lead again before the weekend after we passed the scoring gate of Fernando de Noronha off the coast of Brazil.

Now, as we both negotiate our path around the St Helena High, we're looking good to get another slingshot ahead of the others, thanks to this pretty reliable weather system. Right now, we trail *PRB* by 36 miles on the official race tracker though, with 19,500 miles to go, we're effectively neck and neck.

Astern of us, Roland Jourdain and Jean-Luc Nélias on *Veolia Environment* are more than 250 miles away and sailing slower, as are the others. It's too soon to be sure but we think this margin will quickly multiply over the next few days and both leaders could have a 500-mile lead going into the Southern Ocean towards the next scoring gate south of the Cape of Good Hope.

This will be essential for we have noticed Alex Thompson and Andrew Cape on *Hugo Boss* produce some impressive boat speed earlier when they sailed around *Delta Dore* in breeze. These guys could be a real threat to us in the heavy conditions of the Southern Ocean so we're as well to get ahead while we can.

We've done well so far with the boat in good shape apart from a broken bilge pump and some hydraulic gear that needs attention before we get into the rough stuff. We noticed the bilge pump problem after the forward hatch blew open from the force of water crossing the deck, which then swamped the inside of the boat – we nearly lost all our batteries.

Both J. P. and I have been able to get up to twelve hours of rest per day and our diet has also been a bit more varied than other races I've done when it was strictly freeze-dried from start to finish. Some Spanish ham, bread and biscuits are welcome variations and the added weight that these cost actually helps us. It's not likely to be that way for the next six weeks however, which is how long we expect to be in the Southern Ocean.

It has been an eventful week, for sure, and more to come without doubt. For now I'll sign off with a memory of Steve Fossett whom I was fortunate enough to crew for when we broke the round-the-world speed sailing record on *Cheyenne*. He's been missing for more than three months and the process of declaring him officially dead is under way. It'd be wishful thinking to hope he took off somewhere for a quiet break from the limelight of all his epic adventures. Maybe. But wherever his resting place is, be it the Colorado Desert or a bar in South America, I wish him rest and peace.

South Atlantic: Tristan da Cunha, 37° 4' S 12° 19' W

This island group is one of the most isolated inhabited places on earth, accessible only by sea. This volcanic archipelago was discovered by a Portuguese explorer in 1506, who gave the main island his own name. Today, it is a British Overseas Territory and has about 275 inhabitants who reportedly share just eight surnames between eighty families.

Gough and Inaccessible Islands, 40° 19' S 9° 56' W

The southeasternmost island of the Tristan da Cunha archipelago by 400 miles, deserted other than the weather station staff, the island is an important albatross nesting ground, a UNESCO World Heritage Site and has been described as one of the least disrupted ecosystems of its kind.

In 1968 Bill King, now 101 and living in Galway, was racing the first Golden Globe race, the original of all round-the-world races. King lost radio contact during the race. On 31 October, Galway Blazer II capsized in 50-foot waves northeast of Gough Island while King rested, breaking both masts. King was eventually towed to Cape Town, South Africa.

Log 4

9 December 2007: deep into the Southern Ocean that surrounds Antarctica and the fleet is thinning considerably due to mast and gear failures.

We're a full month and 8,000 miles into the race and we're suddenly into a new game completely. Barely had *PRB* and ourselves entered the Southern Ocean and we regained the overall lead when we found ourselves without our main contender. We were shocked to learn that Vincent Riou and Seb Josse on *PRB* are out of the race as the top section of their rig collapsed on Saturday morning. They were within a few miles of us and, by their own account, hadn't been pushing as hard as we were, which got us ahead. It's an inevitable risk and could strike any of us so there's no gloating over their misfortune. I doubt any of us in the fleet want to win this on the basis of the others being knocked out.

On the other hand, ocean racing is as much a test of humans as it is of design and gear considerations. We've always considered their boat the race pacesetter and as the lads on *PRB* head north to Cape Town, hopefully before the next low-pressure system and its 40-knot winds reach the area, J. P. and I switch our attention to the chasing pack.

Passing south of Gough Island we were first to pass through the fourth scoring gate due south of the Cape of Good Hope and again collected the points for first place, but Alex Thompson and Andrew Cape on *Hugo Boss* have rocketed into form now and are making steady gains as each sked comes in.

This form isn't a surprise: we expected their speed and, fair play to them, they established a new world record for a 60-foot monohull boat with 500 miles sailed in 24 hours – that's an average of 20.83 knots for the period. At least Seb can take some comfort as he heads to Africa from the fact that his outright monohull record of 563 miles set on *ABN AMRO 2* in the last Volvo Race remains intact, for the time being at least.

Hugo Boss may be gaining but they still have Roland 'Bilou' Jourdain and Jean-Luc Nélias on *Veolia Environnement* 40 miles ahead to eliminate first, before another 82 miles to reach us. It sounds like a lot but in the extreme conditions of the Roaring Forties, a small slip by us or even a problem with gear could cost us the lead.

Our job now is to concentrate on positioning ourselves for the best route through the progression of lows heading eastwards. We'll be averaging around 20 knots much of the time so ignoring the wet and freezing cold makes this the toughest stage of the race. Only another month to go!

Meanwhile, *PRB* aren't the only ones with problems to contend with. *Estrella Damm* had a collision of some kind and have damaged one of their rudders. They could take a small penalty and pull in for repairs when we near Australia or New Zealand but so far they look good to continue racing. As for Vincent and Seb heading for Africa, their consolation prize for being knocked out of the race is that they can enjoy Christmas in Cape Town.

Have one for us, boys!

Indian Ocean: Kerguelen Plateau, 49° 15' S 69° 35' E

Also known as the Desolation Islands, the islands and their huge plateau are part of a now submerged subcontinent that was originally joined to India, Australia and Antarctica. The large archipelago was only discovered in 1772. Despite its inhospitable nature with steep-sided mountains, the highest at 1,850 metres, ice fields and fierce katabatic winds that regularly blast the kelp-strewn harbour making it treacherous, it became an important whaling and sealing base. In modern times a weather and scientific base was established there, taking advantage of the island's position deep in the southern Indian Ocean, and it was later used for a time for rocket testing.

Log 5

16 December 2007: still in the South and civilisation couldn't be further away from us anywhere on the planet; approaching the halfway mark.

We're alone now. Very alone. Just J. P. below, resting as *Paprec Virbac* glides steadily across the ocean, closer to Antarctica than anywhere else, but that's hardly appealing as there's a massive ice field surrounding the continent.

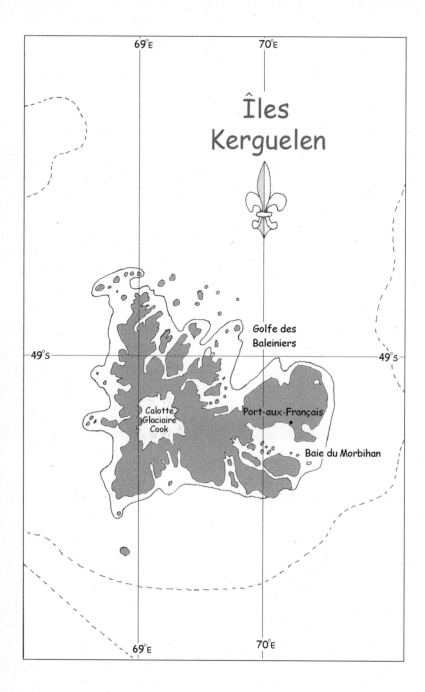

Grey sky, grey sea, the horizon a tenuous line in the middle, broken only by the occasional white cap; it's mesmerising sailing as I alternate between hand-steering and then the autopilot when it's just too cold to continue. We're now so deep into the Southern Ocean that the deep depressions are coming at us almost like a scheduled train service. We must be especially careful not to be caught on the wrong side and get trapped between headwinds and the ice, but for now, thankfully, we've been given a reprieve and we can catch up on rest.

Astern of us, the fleet has taken a hammering in the last week and three of the top boats are now out of the running completely. First to go was *PRB*, our constant match-racing partners up front. Then it was *Delta Dore* with a complete dismasting. The lads on *Estrella Damm* were next with two smashed rudders. A pit stop in Cape Town resulted in repairs to their boat but without time to test the repairs, they too have pulled out of the race. *PRB* being knocked out gave us a clear 250-mile lead to the next placed boat, *Veolia Environnement*. But they've had problems with their engine and diverted to the Kerguelen Islands for repairs and a twelve-hour time penalty.

Jean-Luc on *Veolia Environnement* reported:

After a tricky landing on the island amongst the kelp beds, we threaded a path through the elephant seals that cover the island's coasts. On arrival at the barracks a mechanic was sent for by the base commander to assist with the boat repair. We were given a welcome hot meal of fresh food as the island had just been restocked by a yearly supply ship from La Réunion.

As the repair got under way, Bilou and I had a limited tour of the spectacular surrounds of the base in a beat-up Peugot 205 that had be customized for the environment with doors welded shut and chains welded to the chassis so that it could be attached safely to avoid being blown away during the winter winds. The Peugeot was mandatory in the winter to enable the station crew to get from one building to the next in the hurricane force winds.

With the engine eventually repaired, we left complete with the added irony of picking up two fresh pineapples for our stores, courtesy of the supply ship and we rejoined the race fleet.

They're back in the race again but more than 800 miles behind in third place. That little diversion cost them 500 miles – we can't let that happen to us and thankfully all our gear is holding up well so far.

The incessant movement of sea and sky, it's mind numbing here at almost 55 degrees south – iceberg territory.

And then I see it, incredibly merged into the bland seascape but as we draw closer there can be no mistaking it. It's a berg, about a mile long and perhaps a few hundred metres high.

All hell breaks loose on board as J. P. joins me on deck. We have less than 10 miles to collision but that assumes the berg has no accompanying growlers – chunks of broken ice partially submerged and easily capable of holing us. Ten miles at almost 20 knots – that's half an hour to drop the gennaker, hoist the Solent, alter course and sail around it to avoid impact. We cleared it with 3 miles to spare but what would have happened had it been night time?

It was a nerve-wracking experience and we have held a northeasterly course since it is to a slightly warmer latitude where there is less threat from the ice and will hopefully position us better for the next low-pressure system coursing its merry way eastwards.

That was how Saturday morning started for us. And then the first of the satellite skeds came in with the shocking news that while we were dicing with the berg, to our north Alex Thompson and Andrew Cape on *Hugo Boss* had taken 130 miles out of our lead *in just one night!* We always knew that these guys were fast and their menace has been growing steadily since *PRB* pulled out. We regained a few miles and still have more than a 100-mile 'cushion' between us, which is effectively dead even for the overall lead. It looks like the remainder of our time in the Southern Ocean is going to be a morning routine of dashing to the nav. station for the first report after the twelve-hour blackout period to see if Alex and Capey have pulled another 130-mile stunt or if we have edged ahead.

'Dear Santa . . .'

What followed over Christmas week was a drag race between both boats south of Australia and heading for the Cook Strait. Little did we know that significant rudder issues were persistently affecting Hugo Boss. *They had also*

*accidentally dumped most of their diesel supply into their
bilge during a broach and were running on critically low
power supply. The first we knew of this was when their
shore crew were spotted in significant numbers in Wellington,
giving us a hint something might be up.*

Log 6

23 December 2007: approaching the South Island of New
Zealand and an opportunity to take a pit stop but whether it's
worth a time penalty . . .

More than forty days at sea and we're blasting along nicely
now. There's an palpable air of excitement on board *Paprec
Virbac* as both J. P. and I look forward to seeing civilisation
for the first time in almost three weeks. Not that we'll be
stopping; we have the overall lead to protect and this race
is ours to lose.

Alex Thompson and Andrew Cape on *Hugo Boss* are
sailing a great race and are keeping us under constant
pressure just 100 miles astern as we close on the Cook Strait
between New Zealand's North and South Islands.

We're in a marginally better position since my last
report a week ago when the big black boat was charging up
the Southern Ocean, taking more than 100 miles out of our
hard-earned lead in just one night. During normal daylight
hours (under GMT) we receive two-hourly updates of our
performance. By night, however, a twelve-hour blackout
period is applied and this was a fearful time for us as *Hugo
Boss* finally delivered their potent challenge. In the end, they
came within 12 miles of our lead before the weather front

that brought them up reached us as well and we could fire up the afterburners and extend once again.

But our 100-mile lead is tenuous at best, especially as there will easily be a light-wind zone to the west of New Zealand and they may be slightly better positioned to the northwest to take advantage of this. Currently, we expect to pass through the strait on Christmas Day, hopefully with a two- to six-hour lead on Alex and Capey.

Right now we have 25 to 30 knots of breeze, full mainsail and fairly flat seas with around 1-metre waves. In fact, we haven't really seen anything too big so far, perhaps up to 15 metres but no more.

At the moment, we have a private match-race duel up front as the remaining boats in the race are 1,500 miles and more behind us.

And we could yet lose another competitor if Dominique Wavre and Michelle Paret on *Tenemos II* cannot easily repair the structural damage to their keel when they pull in to Wellington next weekend.

Meanwhile, our December food bag has been completely depleted of tasty treats as we hit the chocolate stuff pretty hard in the tough conditions of the last few weeks. But I'm reliably informed that my Christmas present has some surprises and right now I'm resisting temptation to start unwrapping early.

Being at sea for Christmas isn't new to me and I've forgotten my own birthday and many others plenty of times on one deep-ocean race or another.

But this year is different as I'll be missing Oisín's first Christmas and I would very much like to be there with him and Suzy-Ann. They're having a white Christmas in Canada and I believe Santa is bringing him a sled so there'll be plenty of photos coming by email this week.

We're past this halfway mark and just one more foray into the Southern Ocean to notorious Cape Horn before finally turning northwards in the Atlantic once again. In the meantime, it's back-watching time again as we wait to see if a black hull emerges for another duel.

With best wishes to all for a happy and peaceful Christmas, from everyone on board *Paprec Virbac*.

Pacific Ocean: Chatham Islands 43° 53' S 176° 31' W

Located just 800 kilometres from New Zealand's South Island, this archipelago of ten islands is home to about 650 people. The beauty of the islands disguises its particularly bloody history of genocide in which the indigenous Moriori, a Polynesian tribe who had lived there for hundreds of years as hunter-gatherers and fishermen, were virtually extinguished by a Maori two-tribe invasion in 1835, the population of 2,000 disappeared, cannibalised and slaughtered, or for the remaining women, assimilated into the conquering Maori population.

Log 7

30 December 2007: heading southwards once again, towards iceberg territory and the fastest great circle route to Cape Horn.

Today we will be fifty days at sea and the fourth consecutive week we hold the overall lead. We're well settled into our routine on board but the pressure remains intense. Since Christmas Day when we reached the Cook Strait between New Zealand's North and South islands, we have dived back into the Southern Ocean. Now we're back in the Furious Fifties as we prepare for the next ice gate and the final stage in this starkly beautiful part of the world before we reach Cape Horn.

We're in the lead but this means little. We've effectively started a 10,000-mile race to the finish, which will be a survival test for us while Alex Thompson and Andrew Cape on *Hugo Boss* are in hot pursuit with a revamped boat. Their 48-hour pit stop in Wellington allowed us to build a 927-mile lead, about two and half days, but already they're eating into this and yesterday took 150 miles off this with sustained boat speeds of more than 20 knots. Still, we've done well and are in good shape considering we haven't stopped and incurred time penalties.

Well, that's not strictly correct. We have had a mini pit stop after we collided with an object last week that took a chunk of outer skin off our starboard rudder. Because these Open 60s have twin rudders, they're more susceptible to damage as they lack the protection of the keel.

We could have risked continuing in the race and chances are the rudder would have been okay – just. But we opted for a mini unofficial stop to inspect the damage and the rest of the boat. We considered pulling into the Chatham Islands but with a high pressure threatening to engulf us, we instead hove to at sea as we quickly tended to the repairs. It was an investment of sorts, sacrificing some of the lead for peace of mind.

I've covered the damaged area with a new skin to avoid water getting into the carbon fibre of the rudder and delaminating it, so it's fine now. I've also been halfway up the rig but after 15,000 miles have yet to complete a full climb and inspection! We're pretty happy it's okay but it is something we need to address before too long.

Overall, we've done well on the damage list. Just a blown-out jammer (deck fitting) and various running repairs, mostly sails, that have kept me busy. Nevertheless, in Formula One terms, *Hugo Boss* has had a full pit stop and a retune; on board *Paprec Virbac*, we're fighting to the finish.

Our routine is still three hours on watch and three hours off for rest. In between, gybing involves both of us preparing the boat and sails for the manoeuvre, which is intensely physical and will be even more so in the freezing conditions of the Deep South. It may be a routine but it's critical for us now. We are able to sail at 100 per cent but to maintain our lead, every move we make leads to intense discussions between J. P. and myself, especially as we dodge the progression of low-pressure systems rolling eastwards. If we get it wrong, we could end up with 40 to 50 knots of wind and mountainous waves, which will slow us. And Francis Joyon on *IDEC 2* who has separately embarked on a record-breaking solo circumnavigation has reported icebergs in our original route, which is why the ice gate has been shifted to the north for safety. In truth, these diversions don't completely stop the fleet from going into ice territory as the shortest route eastward is always furthest south, which is exactly where we try and sail for after clearing each gate.

We have around one week to get to Cape Horn. Our ideal scenario would be to build and maintain a 1,000-mile lead, which would leave us very happy for the final approach up the South Atlantic and then to Barcelona.

The last satellite report of the day has just arrived in. Alex and Capey are charging now and are 755 miles astern of us as we slow ahead of the next weather system. They're to the north and may yet make more gains so the next forty-eight hours will be especially crucial. Their pit stop may have given us a boost and changed our perspective but our objective remains the same: we must still reach Barcelona before we can win this race.

Log 8

6 January 2008: alone and leading still, an end to the rigour of the Southern Ocean is within sight and warmer weather too.

Almost there! Just 1,000 miles to run before we reach Cape Horn and the South Atlantic once again. We're still a long way from home and the finishing line off Barcelona but the exit from the Southern Ocean will be a welcome relief to J. P. and myself after an intense passage around this wild and exposed expanse.

But if the stress of dodging icebergs and vicious weather is at last gone, we'll have plenty of new concerns before the final quarter of this contest is decided. At least we won't be like a tourist boat, tripping around huge bergs and tiny lumps of ice but we are getting very little sleep as we try to keep the pace up.

Astern of us, Alex Thompson and Andrew Cape on *Hugo Boss* continue to pace us like a tracking tiger, waiting for us to slip up and pounce on the overall lead. The nearer we get to the finish, the fewer opportunities there are to recover from such a scenario. Right now, they're hanging on to us about 750 miles behind and last week's notion of getting a 1,000-mile safety blanket between us by Cape Horn is clearly now a pipe dream; the elastic between us remains tight.

We lost around 130 miles over the weekend as we were stuck in a transition zone between low-pressure systems and our speed dropped to less than 10 knots as we ploughed upwind while *Hugo Boss* is still piling down to the Horn at top speed. Nevertheless, we do have a full weather system between us and while we expect to ride this depression the whole way to the Horn, the lads on *Hugo Boss* have only caught the tail end of their system so hopefully this will stop them making more significant gains.

But we too have concerns about getting past the cape despite the fact that it's summertime and we hope to have the weather with us. And beyond there, the passage northwards past the Falkland Islands could see our lead eroded if we hit light conditions as Francis Joyon on his solo non-stop record attempt with his catamaran *IDEC 2* discovered last week.

In truth, if we can hold this lead, we won't really be happy until we reach the equator later this month because after this, the only people who can beat us will be ourselves by making a tactical slip-up or having a technical problem.

As far as the latter goes, we are much happier now as the calm conditions sailing through the ice fields last week allowed plenty of time to give the boat a very thorough check-up. And I had finally managed to complete a full rig-climb, the first since starting the race nearly two months

246

ago! From the masthead, as far as the eye could see we were surrounded by chunks of ice of different sizes. That inspection was very reassuring to us. I was able to rerun a spinnaker halyard and also protect one of the mast runners that was looking a little bit worn. I also reinforced the port rudder bracket that is worse for wear, so on the whole we're pretty happy with our running repairs.

Overall, with less than a month to go, we have a full-on race going between *Paprec Virbac* and *Hugo Boss*. J. P. and I may have a 750-mile ace card but there's little else that might assure us of the overall victory.

We are in our routine of sailing fast and hard, sail changes, keeping watch, grabbing rest, sail changes, more sail changes and poring over the latest weather data, which will see us doing more of the same for the final 7,500 miles.

Cape Horn: Le Maire Strait, 54° 50' S 64° 55' W

If Cape Horn has captured the popular imagination as a place of maritime achievement, Le Maire Strait is itself a difficult passage with quickly changing, often gale force, winds and currents that reach over 8 knots. It is synonymous with all those who have had to navigate past the infamous headland that separates the Pacific and Atlantic oceans. The strait is Argentine-controlled while the cape itself is Chilean, the result of both countries' independence from Spain in the early nineteenth century but only after protracted claims of sovereignty by the states.

Isla de los Estados, 54° 45' S 63° 53' W

Also known as Staten Island, the island is an impressive

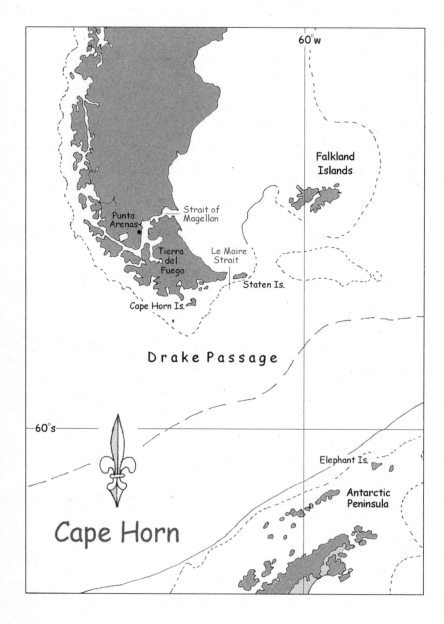

60°w

Falkland
Islands

Strait of
Magellan

Punta
Arenas

Tierra
del
Fuego

Le Maire
Strait

Staten Is.

Cape Horn Is.

Drake Passage

60°s

Elephant Is.

Antarctic
Peninsula

Cape Horn

fortress of cliffs and unprotected bays. Classified as a nature reserve, it is also a major cause for seamen to celebrate as it marks the turn out of the Southern Ocean and into the Atlantic. As the southeastern boundary to Le Maire Strait, typically in a round-the-world race the next decision is whether to sail up the coast of Argentina or northeast to the Falkland Islands. If coming from Europe and heading westbound, the choice is more likely to be whether to head into the weather or seek shelter somewhere along the Beagle Channel close to Ushuaia.

Log 9

13 January 2008: nip and tuck northwards in the South Atlantic and the race is ours to lose.

So here we are, sitting off the coast of Argentina, heading north and getting warmer by the day. We have less than 6,000 miles to sail, a quarter of this race remaining, out of the icy Southern Ocean, we're in the lead still and have a fairly comfortable 850-mile advantage over *Hugo Boss* who remain our sole rivals.

And yet the stress levels are at their maximum, the worst yet with the outcome of this race hanging in the balance, at the mercy of the wind gods as I feel the pit of my stomach tightening by the day. Since rounding Cape Horn last Thursday morning, there has been no let-up. Getting past it and then negotiating Le Maire Strait between Tierra del Fuego and Staten Island took an immense amount of energy as we kept the pace on. It has eaten into our energy levels and sapped us as we constantly trim and re-trim the boat, changing sails, resetting sheets, taking in and then letting out the reef slabs in the mainsail as each wind shift blows in.

We cannot allow our game to slip, not now, not after we have achieved so much between holding the lead and avoiding damage to our boat and gear. I managed to climb the rig again and just a fractional halyard was showing signs of chafe so that's been changed now and hopefully we've avoided a problem at a more crucial time later on.

The exhaustion of the past week has failed to diminish our spirits and within a few days we should be enjoying more tropical sailing as we head for the second-last scoring gate at Fernando de Noronha off Brazil where we will complete our circumnavigation.

And yet we watch and wait to see what way the weather breaks for Alex and Capey as they clear the Horn and start northwards in the South Atlantic. Here's how the next week or ten days will play out: dominating the tactical game is the question of how to tackle the St Helena high-pressure system that usually persists between South America and Africa. This can mostly deliver steady if light conditions northwards to the equator and is generally tackled by sailing west of the Falklands. On the other hand, in previous races such as the Volvo Ocean Race or before that, the Whitbread, a stopover port in Uruguay or Brazil would normally see us duck west of the Falklands for the most direct route up the coast. However, we were obliged to take this course last Friday as a massive depression west of South Georgia would have delivered 50-plus knots that would surely have tested our gear to its limits, possibly beyond.

Instead, we began tacking into the wind off the coast and, while it's not our fastest point of sail, we made reasonable progress as *Hugo Boss* surged into the Cape and reduced our lead from 1,000 miles to 800 before they too slowed and we opened ground again. At least my previous hopes of a 1,000-mile lead at the cape proved not to be a pipe dream after all.

The problem now is that while we have opted for a more coastal route and should have breeze for a few days yet, there is more of a chance that it could crap out on us altogether as we close on Brazil and the warmer latitudes. If Alex and Capey take a flyer and head offshore, they may well have us.

We can certainly expect to see our lead cut back to a few hundred miles by the time we reach Fernando and even then I won't start to be truly happy until we have got through the doldrums on the other side of the equator.

There's only a couple of weeks of racing left in this contest. We may even reach Barcelona by the end of the month. But if you were to offer to shorten the course to just 20 miles ahead of us right now, I think I'd probably take you up on the offer. Until then, I'll have the wooden batten firmly clenched between my teeth as this final stage is played out.

South Atlantic Ocean: Trinidade & Martim Vaz, 20° 31' S 29° 19' W

The haul northwards up the Atlantic towards warmer climes is marked by the six volcanic islands in the Trindade and Martim Vaz chain. They were discovered in 1502 by the Portuguese navigator Estêvão da Gama and were subject to various claims of sovereignty and possession over the years, eventually to become Brazilian flagged. Steeped in maritime legend, the islands were mentioned in Richard Henry Dana's classic book Two Years before the Mast *and, in 1781, were the site of a shipwreck that averted loss of life thanks to a display of seamanship that has become part of sea-faring lore.* HMS Rattlesnake *had intended to carry out a survey of the islands for the India trading companies and had anchored for the night. But as the wind increased after dark, the 198-ton 12-gun cutter-rigged sloop started to drag so that by morning, the cable on one of their two anchors snapped. Rattlesnake's commander ordered sails to be set and managed to swing back out to sea on the second anchor. But in unknown waters, she struck a submerged rock and began to sink. To preserve life, she was run ashore where all hands were saved and rescued three months later by a convoy passing by chance.*

More recently, the islands came to public attention in France in 1968 when Bernard Moitessier sailed into the bay after abandoning his attempt at winning the Golden Globe Race to become the first person to sail solo, non-stop around the world. The race was ultimately won by Robin Knox-Johnson on Suhaili *and not long after, inspired by the success of the contest, the Whitbread Round-the-World Race started.*

Log 10

20 January 2008: warmth at last plus 'champagne sailing', as a taste of what lies ahead.

At last! Finally, we have reached the trade winds off the coast of Brazil and we can look forward to improving conditions over the next week. Still up front, still in the lead and still with a good margin over *Hugo Boss* in pursuit.

Last week's log predicted our lead would drop to just a few hundred miles and our previous 1,000 miles has indeed been halved as expected. But my mood a week ago was born of stress and it took the arrival of the trades for our outlook to improve. Alex Thompson and Andrew Cape are hot on our heels, currently around 550 miles astern, but that's as close as they've got. No sign of a risky flyer deep into the Atlantic by them, thankfully, as they've opted to cover our track and await a weather break.

They almost got it when a depression delivered fast reaching conditions for the big black boat while the same weather system saw us beating upwind. But we've just punched through a semi-stationary cold front and now it's their turn.

We spent the last week punching through big seas with waves that just got rougher and rougher as we jumped from crest to crest. In the end, we carried on with reduced sail area rather than become exhausted from constant changes. It was hard on us till Friday when the gale started to ease. So bad in fact that I managed only one phone call home and just a couple of emails.

On the other side is warmer weather and though initially it's more slow, upwind work, the breeze is steady and soon we'll be able to free off for slightly faster reaching angles as we head up to the scoring gate at Fernando de Noronha about a thousand miles away – the weekend at the latest.

The improved weather has lifted our spirits enormously. The layers of clothing are being peeled off and tomorrow I expect to be trading in my sea boots for deck shoes. It's going to be shorts and T-shirt sailing for sure but the rum 'n' cokes will have to wait until Barcelona.

As the miles to the finish are ticking away with just over 4,000 remaining, our thoughts and discussions centre more and more on keeping the boat together as the tactical options rely simply on staying ahead and moving forward. *Hugo Boss* on the other hand will face fewer and fewer chances to get ahead of us and will be relying on gear failure for us for that to happen. At the end of the day we have to keep in mind that our boat has been sailing non-stop since the start while they have had a two-day pit stop and mini-refit.

Here's how we expect the next week or so to play out: on current pace, we expect to be ahead by a similar distance when we reach Fernando de Noronha and the completion of our circumnavigation. After this, the doldrums beckon once more but at this time of year and for a northbound crossing, we don't expect this to be too much of a drama. We will probably slow considerably and hopefully, if we are becalmed, it won't be for very long. Once into the North Atlantic, another tactical choice presents itself, which could be the last major opportunity for *Hugo Boss* to jump ahead or into a challenging position. Option A would be to retrace our earlier track and sail up the coast of Africa past the Canary Islands. Definitely shorter but will there be a breeze? As it's against the prevailing wind it usually has less of a breeze. Option B would be to continue north on the classic route, almost as far as the Azores before turning in towards Madeira and then to the Strait of Gibraltar and the (probably) light stage up to Barcelona.

That decision is still two weeks away and before then, we must keep moving, keep the boat together and keep ticking off the miles. We have just enough food, gas and diesel for three weeks and our game is simply to keep ahead of Alex and Capey and be ahead when they get their last throw of the dice.

Atlantic equator: St Peter & St Paul Rocks, 00° 55' N 029° 20' W

Fernando de Noronha has become well known in ocean racing as a scoring gate or the halfway point along the Atlantic stage of a round-the-world race. However, an even smaller archipelago of islets and rocks is located a further 625 kilometres to the northeast in the doldrums region. First discovered 500 years ago, when a Portuguese naval expedition to India crashed into the rocks at night, today just four Brazilian scientists live there, operating a research station on fortnightly shifts. It is the second-largest megamullion (oceanic core complex) in the world and the only location on earth where the abyssal mantle is exposed above sea level.

Log 11

27 January 2008: fifty days in the lead, non-stop. We arrive back to cross our outbound track off Brazil and can head for home.

As we celebrate fifty consecutive days in the lead of the race, two major firsts took place over the last week. Both were very welcome though a certain amount of trepidation was involved with one and the other, well, what can I say but it was about time that it happened.

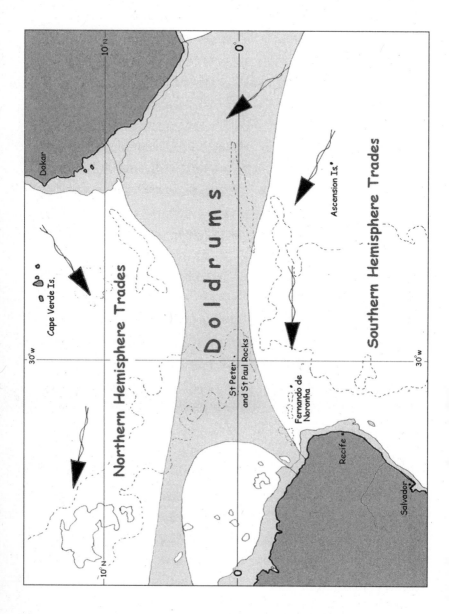

We reached the Fernando de Noronha scoring gate off the northeast coast of Brazil and shortly afterwards made our second crossing in this race of the equator. As we began our battle with the doldrums, emerging from this tricky zone allowed us to think for the first time about the finish line now just over 2,500 miles away. Until now, we haven't allowed ourselves to get either excited or become distracted about the prospect of completing this 25,000-mile marathon; there's too much at stake before then. It has simply been a case of sailing two stages at a time, the current one and then positioning ourselves for the next part. But that's over now and we have got to start thinking about reaching Barcelona – it's that close! Next Monday's log could be the last of this race and it all comes down to the breeze in the North Atlantic.

True, we have managed to keep our lead over Alex Thompson and Andrew Cape on *Hugo Boss*. We even saw it build to almost 900 miles. Although we were prepared for it to happen, they never did manage to breach the 500-mile barrier and close to within a few hundred miles, though that may yet happen. Right now, they've been experiencing what we went through at the start of last week, slogging upwind and, though they've freed off a bit and gained on us while we were in the doldrums, they too will have to face this zone so the lead could open up yet again.

Yet I'm still not certain about what will happen to us in the North Atlantic. There's lots of potential for the lead to be eaten away and while we are thinking more and more about the finish, it's still a considerable distance off.

With *Hugo Boss* so far behind, there's no way we can

consider covering tactics so our strategy remains two-fold: (1) keep the boat moving, clicking off the miles towards the finish and (2) keep the boat intact though it's going to be hard as it'll be mostly upwind to Gibraltar. We think it'll be less than ten days of sailing left and while we're pretty happy with our food and diesel rationing, we're by no means flush and can't simply switch on the autopilot or the Fleet (satellite communications) whenever we feel like it.

But sailing in these warm latitudes and calm conditions means we can stand longer watch routines and get more maintenance done off watch than before. When it's warm, the whole boat comes alive and cleaning is an essential chore.

Which leads me to the second first from the last week and an admission really. In spite of frequent applications of baby wipes and soap under full thermals and oilskins, the last week also saw my first proper wash since leaving Barcelona seventy-five days ago. We've just been a bit too busy really. Hopefully, time will allow for a few more of these before we reach the dock as I'm not quite sure what Suzy-Ann and especially Oisín would make of the *Paprec Virbac* version of L'Air du Temps.

Madeira: Desertas Islands, 32° 32' N 16° 31' W

Hiding just south of the Madeiran islands, a chain of three long and narrow islands that stretch over a distance of 23 kilometres north–south are deserted except for a ranger's home to supervise activity around the islands, which are a protected nature reserve. Spectacular rock formations are layered through the steep volcanic rock of the islands' faces.

Log 12

3 February 2008: almost three months at sea and we're down to the last of our food and gas supplies. And the treats are all gone too!

We're now more than eighty-four days at sea, exactly the maximum duration that we budgeted for in our fuel, food and gas supplies but thankfully we prepared for a longer trip so we're not in bad shape with less than 1,000 miles to reach the Strait of Gibraltar. Astern of us as usual, the men in black on *Hugo Boss* are just beyond striking distance at over 500 miles but remain a threat to us as does gear failure on our own tiring boat. But we've kept moving forward in the last week, picked up some good breeze and we've enjoyed nice sunny conditions.

We're pretty happy with where they are right now and even our lead should be enough to deal with the inevitable slowdowns that we'll meet. Thankfully, neither of us went for the African coast (the shorter route), which would have meant bashing upwind for the remainder of the race. As it is, every wave we lift off ends with a sickening crash and is a constant worry for us as the loads on the boat and rig from this are tremendous.

Overnight, we were expecting the breeze to go light again as a high-pressure system rolls over our position but for the early part of this week, we're looking at fresh sou'westerlies to bring us up to Cabo São Vicente off Portugal before going light again on the approach to Gibraltar when it'll be upwind sailing again. After that, well, it's fairly unpredictable. There's a chance we might get lucky and hold the breeze all or most of the way to the finish. But there's also a good chance of finding a great big parking lot in the Med that will be tricky and will end the race as it started.

Our lead will stand to us well for this scenario but compression within the fleet or at least amongst the front runners is quite likely. But the nearer we get to the end and our gap ahead of *Hugo Boss* remains the same, the less likely their chances of catching us and the biggest threat to our victory will be gear failure; if we lose after all we've been through we're going to be pretty disappointed.

Overall, around 1,500 miles to go and we should be finished at Barcelona by 11 February and getting excited is tempting but might be a waste of energy – we have food but it's thin on the ground and while we'll last, it won't be by much and it certainly won't be three-course lunches either. On a race like this, the nice food gets eaten first and the second choices slip further back down the bags until they're all that's left. I'm pretty sick of freeze-dried rice pudding with apple and cinnamon and if I never eat it again, it will be no bad thing.

But having no snacks left and coming off watch to grab a quick meal of nuts or biscuits or something isn't on and instead the drudgery of boiling up water, soaking the freeze-fried food and then cooking it is soul-destroying when you're exhausted after being on watch for four hours and gasping for sleep.

Astern of us, Alex and Capey were able to fully re-provision *Hugo Boss* during their pit stop in Wellington. Fine for those guys but we wouldn't trade with them – snacks and DVD movies are for pussies and miles in the lead is where it's really at! Well, maybe some Mars bars as well wouldn't be too bad. These I miss, a lot. J. P. managed to keep his stores going till last week when he had his last Mars. It must have been my sideways glance as he unwrapped it that made him share which is a great sign that we're still getting on well after three months at sea. The alternative – winch handles at dawn –is unthinkable.

The thought of finishing the race is starting to loom large. After last week's bout of hygiene, we've become aware of just how smelly the boat is down below with just two of us living in such a cramped space. For me, my major decision is whether or not to shave. Just shaving stubble is easy enough but the full beard is going to be a right pain in the ass. I know Suzy-Ann won't mind and I hope it won't scare Oisín but right now I'm resisting.

Still, three months at sea is definitely showing in other areas as well. I'm not quite sure how but the line of a song has somehow lodged itself inside my head and for the last two weeks seems to appear around about the first hour of my watch. Every night, regular as clockwork, Dolly Parton blares into my mind with 'One day at a time, sweet Jesus . . .'

Strait of Gibraltar: Isla de Perejil (Parsley Island), 35° 55' N 05° 25' W

This little known and tiny rocky island, located just 250 metres off the Moroccan coast, is disputed territory close to the autonomous North African Spanish city of Ceuta on the south side of the Strait of Gibraltar. Measuring just 480 square metres, it had been used for centuries by farmers

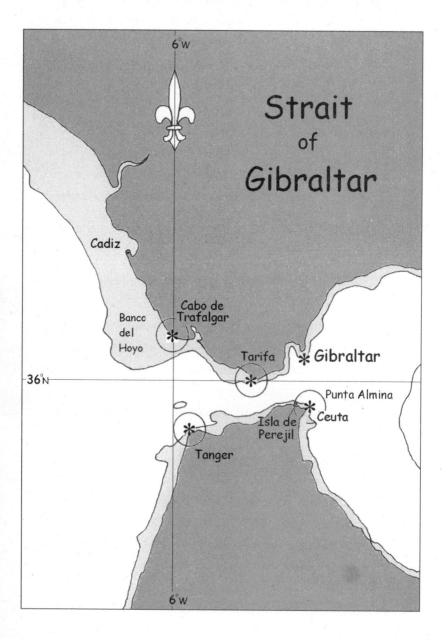

until a small detachment of young Moroccan cadets started some exercises there, displacing an old woman and her goats. Spain's exaggerated reaction to the 'invasion' sent commando forces with full navy and air force support to occupy the islet. The cadets offered no resistance and were taken to Ceuta before being released after a truce was brokered by US Secretary of State Colin Powell. Perejil has been deserted by goats and all ever since.

Log 13

10 February 2008: Back inside the Med and we complete the 'technical' circumnavigation. Just the finishing line to go . . .

That's it – we've done it! Not won the race, mind, just done the circumnavigation past the three Capes (Good Hope, Leeuwin and Horn) on the classic route around the planet. We're almost home and the waves of a stormy passage past Gibraltar have been replaced by waves of expectation as we come to terms with what lies just ahead in Barcelona. Fewer than 300 miles to go, light airs the whole way and a good thing too. But more of that shortly. In truth, J. P. and I are breathing a huge sigh of relief. Gulping it down in fact, even though we're still not there yet so we're crossing everything – fingers, toes the lot!

The last week has seen painfully slow progress as we battled against headwinds. In fact, we were obliged to sail too far north, as far up as the Azores, in order to keep moving and not get becalmed in the centre of a high-pressure system over the Canaries. And all the time, Alex and Capey on *Hugo Boss* were slowly reeling us in, clipping off the DTL (distance to leader), thanks to a better wind angle that gave them faster reaching conditions compared to our upwind slog.

Then we finally turned eastwards, in past the Algarve coast and as we closed on Gibraltar and the gateway to the Mediterranean, the wind started to blow and blow until we had a full gale on our hands and nasty, short, steep waves piling out into the Atlantic making our path ahead torturous.

I've sailed in this part of the world many times before and I have never seen it this bad; truckloads of wind and consistently so for days. Even after we passed Gib and the scoring gate, it continued, so we ducked in towards the Spanish coast where we tacked along in relative shelter until we passed the worst of the gale.

In fact, since Gibraltar, we've tacked thirty-two times! In a fully crewed boat or a dinghy, this is normally a pretty simple 'ready-about, lee-ho' and all that. Racing an Open 60-footer two-handed is somewhat different. Each tack, where the heading of the boat changes from one side of the wind to the other, takes us about thirty minutes by the time we shift sails and get the boat ready for the new course. It's exhausting multiplied by thirty-two.

Now that the wind has eased, we've moved into deeper water and over to the coast of Algeria for our next tack up towards Ibiza in the reverse of the start three months ago in almost matching conditions.

The easier conditions meant we could be distracted by the France v. Ireland rugby match on Saturday afternoon. Luc and Laurent on our shore team sent us a blow-by-blow account of the game by text and in the second half, I really felt like it was in Ireland's grasp, but in the end the French celebrated a five-point winning margin. We're very happy to be in light winds because for the past two weeks we've been keeping quiet about an incident that nearly ended our race – and still could.

We were off Brazil, bashing through the gale-force squalls of a cold front with *Hugo Boss* starting to gain ground on us when there was a huge bang as the forestay, which is one of the key supports for our mast, broke just above deck level when six tonnes of load became too much for the tired rig. The headsail we had up on the forestay started flailing around in the gusts and, with the heavy furling drum at the bottom, became like a medieval mace as it bashed around, tearing lumps out of the sails and banging into the mast that was thankfully still standing – just – thanks to the baby-stay.

J. P. was on the helm and quickly spun the boat around so we were sailing downwind, which took the pressure off the rig, and yelled for me to come on deck.

It was treacherous. The sail was in bits and unusable but still up and threatened to knock me overboard. It took hours but eventually we were able to jury-rig the mast and forestay, which it is today, lashed down but taking terrific punishment as we crash off wave after wave. It was truly a 'red moment'.

Then twelve hours later we had a problem with our ballast scoop that required J. P. to take a trip overboard for repairs. Other than that, we have a fitting on our mainsail that's coming loose but manageable. After nursing our rig and boat upwind for 6,000 miles through the South and

North Atlantic, we just need the rig to stay up for another 300 miles.

But that's it, the hardest bit is over now. All our pre-race plans and preparations are coming to fruition. We've tried to anticipate as many eventualities as possible, even down to keeping personal areas within our tiny, communal living space on *Paprec Virbac*.

Whatever happens on Monday night, J. P. and I will be lifelong friends. We have come so far, realised an ambition to race around the world against the odds and come home safely. We're now, finally starting to feel proud. Proud to be leading this race, with the Irish and French flags flying together, on the last day at sea before we meet our families and friends again in Barcelona.

Now, where's that razor and shaving-cream?

◄○►

What the log didn't mention that we had just had our first argument that dominated life on board for all of fifteen minutes. After three months at sea, the longest ever for me and living non-stop with just one other person in shared solitary confinement, we each dropped our guard and slipped into a heated debate just half a mile off the coast of Morocco on our final approach to Gibraltar.

The row was about a straightforward choice. The wind was building towards storm force – 50 knots – and though the seas were relatively flat in the shelter of the coast, continuing this close in would mean a series of tacks. Or we could head offshore, but this would mean reducing sail further from the two reefs in the mainsail and a staysail. It really didn't matter which option we took, just so long as we took one. Within half an hour, we would be in bigger wind so the decision was needed.

But we began talking around the issue. Ordinarily, I enjoy a good debate, laying out the logic of the various pros and cons, but this time we needed a clear and quick decision. However, J. P. is a master of dogged persuasiveness and the pair of us kicked off a battle of wills. Yet we had successfully avoided this until now.

Previously, our differences managed to remain always to the point, and from the earliest days even sorting out our normal personality differences came down to an objective discussion that hinged on having the same goal – without that common thread, we could easily have slipped into rancour. In a team environment, differences such as mannerisms and personal habits must be set aside, especially in such confinement. Luckily, J. P. is a hugely personable guy and easy to get along with so we never had an issue living together, and from sailing together before and the qualification race, we were both well inoculated against each other's quirks. But for technical and strategic decisions, we relied massively on analysis of each aspect of the project and sharing of ideas fully. The theory is that if both individuals concur then close to 100 per cent confidence goes into the decision. If both people have different opinions of a decision then care is needed. Our argument was a not-so-subtle example of what could go wrong and threaten the team.

Eventually a decision was made and we tacked inshore again. I ate my humble pie as the wind dropped down to 10 knots and we slowed. He had his vindication but it was short-lived, as we were both happy to have delayed the heavy conditions we eventually found on reaching the axis of the Strait of Gibraltar, and the seas piled higher and higher as the howling wind funnelled through the narrow channel between Europe and North Africa. The ice melted between us as we reported our position to Tarifa Radio. The operator welcomed us back and tentatively offered congratulations but there was still much sailing to be done and losing the rig was the nightmare outcome that we couldn't discount. We knew we were both tired and very stressed.

As we slowly hauled our way into the Med, *Hugo Boss* was gaining ground but would endure even more severe conditions than the 50-knot storm we had. Somewhere in the distance, we allowed, the fat lady was warming up and pretty soon she might even be performing for us. As we sailed northwards, the winds continued to ease until our final night when we made our approach to Barcelona. There – somewhere against the spectacular cityscape and street lighting – lay the finish line and crossing it in the right direction was critical. The first we could properly tell that we had finished and won the race was the yells and cheers from the fleet of small chase boats and the horn from the official boat on the line. We hugged one another and leapt about the deck, almost as much in relief as celebration and thanks.

The shore team boarded us and, as our last port of call was Barcelona, there was no need for the customs declaration. We motored in towards the port and the dockside where we would light hand flares for the traditional arrival and welcome ceremony. Somewhere in the crowd of boats I had spotted Suzy-Ann and expected her to join me on board. But she was with my father on a small RIB with other friends. Oisín had been left ashore with Robert and Patrick who were having their parenting skills tested by a smelly nappy.

But outside, in the darkness and without lights, Suzy-Ann's boat had broken down and stopped in the port channel as a massive car ferry steamed out towards the Med. Their skipper frantically tried to restart the engine, succeeding with only minutes to spare before they would have been run down by the ship. None of us on board *Paprec Virbac* knew about this until another RIB towed them up to us and she and Dad jumped on board.

As we approached the dock after three months at sea the impact of the huge crowd hit us. Friends had travelled from Kerry and sailing mates had driven down from the America's Cup venue in Valencia to greet us. There were more Kerry colours than our sponsors' flags in the crowd but it was the number of friends that took me by surprise. They had a huge Kerry flag and were waving it front of the cameras; it may as well have been our very own day in Croke Park for an All-Ireland final. Oisín was passed up the dock and into my arms. Bewildered by the noise and the crowd, he became upset so I took him inside to the pilot house for some shelter. He was not even a year old; we had only known each other for five months and both needed some time alone. Suzy-Ann came and joined us and, in the heat of the moment, away from the cameras and spotlights, the three of us were together again.

Epilogue

Only a couple of days later, we returned to Kerry as a family. En route, we had stopped in Dublin with J. P. and the team to be received by President Mary McAleese at Áras an Uachtaráin in the Phoenix Park. And on arrival in Caherdaniel, a special welcome ceremony and celebration organised by Helen Wilson marked the achievement of winning another round-the-world race and I was as proud as ever to be a Kerryman.

The next morning was clear and bright like a day in summer though it was not yet springtime. We had gathered at Robert and Sarah's family house perched atop a small hill close to the harbour and offering 360-degree views from its light-filled rooms. Gleaming white sand, windswept clear of footprints and rippling with patterns from the breaking waves, called out for company. After Patrick's culinary speciality – a huge cooked breakfast – heavy coats, hats and gloves were donned and an expeditionary party complete with Suzy-Ann carrying Oisín in his Karrimor set off for a march around Derrynane beach with a football and a throwing-stick for the dog. A few miles of a walk followed by pints and hot lamb sandwiches at Bridie's pub across the road: perfect.

Climbing up past the small saltwater inlet sheltered by the beach, the group scaled a sand dune embankment. In the distance, in the middle of the flooded inlet, four sticks poked skywards, unmoved since two pairs of brothers set them there decades earlier. By now the banter was flowing, thick and fast so it wasn't quite clear who pushed who first but there was a roar, then a scuffle and next the four of us vanished suddenly over the edge of the path and down the side of the sandy cliff face of the dune. Oisín peered out of his Karrimor, craning his neck to see where his dad had just disappeared to. The girls exchanged patient glances as if to say 'boys will be always be boys'.

In the distance, the Atlantic thundered, its great breaking waves pounding against Abbey Island's impassive rocky shoreline that sheltered the beach and its cemetery's panoramic view stretching from Bunavalla around past the harbour and to the beach, giving protection and safety to the inlet.

And still the sea calls, its next ocean-race challenge awaits. Yet the place called home will always remain, unchanged and forever.

Appendix

Round-the-World Races

Barcelona World Race is a non-stop, round-the-world yacht race for crews of two, sailed on Open 60 IMOCA monohull boats. Following the traditional clipper route, it starts and finishes in Barcelona and is held every four years. The first race was staged in 2007–2008.

BOC Round-the-World Race was established in 1982 and was also inspired by the Golden Globe Race as a round-the-world, single-handed yacht race. Briefly known as the Around Alone, it is now known as the Velux 5 Oceans (see below).

Golden Globe Race was a non-stop, single-handed yacht race held in 1968–1969 and was the first round-the-world yacht race.

Jules Verne Trophy: originally conceived in 1990, the Jules Verne is a race against the clock for the fastest circumnavigation of the world by any type of yacht. There are no restrictions on the size of the crew provided the vessel has registered with the organisation and paid an entry fee.

The Race was a non-stop, no-limits race around the world on fully crewed maxi multihulls in the year 2000, beginning and ending in Barcelona to mark the start of the new millenium.

Velux 5 Oceans is a round-the-world, single-handed yacht race, sailed in stages on Open 60-footers and has been managed by Clipper Ventures PLC since 1995. Formerly known as the BOC Challenge (see above), it is sailed every four years.

Vendée Globe is a round-the-world single-handed race, sailed non-stop and without assistance every four years in IMOCA Open 60-footers. First held in 1989, it starts and finishes in Les Sables-d'Olonne in the Vendée département of France.

Volvo Ocean Race is a yacht race sailed in stages on purpose-built Volvo Open 70-footers with a crew of eleven professional sailors and held every three years. It is named after its current owner, which bought the event from Whitbread (see below) in 2001.

Whitbread Round-the-World Race: inspired by the Golden Globe Race, in 1972 Whitbread PLC and the British Royal Naval Sailing Association organised a fully crewed race in stages, based on the route of the traditional square-rigged tall ships.